Pocket
KRAKÓW

TOP SIGHTS · LOCAL LIFE · MADE EASY

Mark Baker

In This Book

QuickStart Guide

Your keys to understanding the city – we help you decide what to do and how to do it

Need to Know
Tips for a smooth trip

Neighbourhoods
What's where

Explore Kraków

The best things to see and do, neighbourhood by neighbourhood

Top Sights
Make the most of your visit

Local Life
The insider's city

The Best of Kraków

The city's highlights in handy lists to help you plan

Best Walks
See the city on foot

Kraków's Best...
The best experiences

Survival Guide

Tips and tricks for a seamless, hassle-free city experience

Getting Around
Travel like a local

Essential Information
Including where to stay

Our selection of the city's best places to eat, drink and experience:

◎ **Sights**

✖ **Eating**

◖ **Drinking**

✪ **Entertainment**

🔒 **Shopping**

These symbols give you the vital information for each listing:

☏ Telephone Numbers	👪 Family-Friendly
⊙ Opening Hours	🐾 Pet-Friendly
🅿 Parking	🚌 Bus
⊖ Nonsmoking	⛴ Ferry
@ Internet Access	Ⓜ Metro
🛜 Wi-Fi Access	🚋 Tram
✗ Vegetarian Selection	🚆 Train
📖 English-Language Menu	

Find each listing quickly on maps for each neighbourhood:

Bar Hemingway

16 🚌 Map p233, B2

Legend has it that Hemi self, wielding a machine rate this timber-pan ered bar during showpiece is a en by Papa ar town. Dress s.com; Hôtel Rit ⊙6.30pm-2a

---

Lonely Planet's Kraków

Lonely Planet Pocket Guides are designed to get you straight to the heart of the city.

Inside you'll find all the must-see sights, plus tips to make your visit to each one really memorable. We've split the city into easy-to-navigate neighbourhoods and provided clear maps so you'll find your way around with ease. Our expert authors have searched out the best of the city: walks, food, nightlife and shopping, to name a few. Because you want to explore, our 'Local Life' pages will take you to some of the most exciting areas to experience the real Kraków.

And of course you'll find all the practical tips you need for a smooth trip: itineraries for short visits; how to get around, and how much to tip the guy who serves you a drink at the end of a long day's exploration.

It's your guarantee of a really great experience.

Our Promise

You can trust our travel information because Lonely Planet authors visit the places we write about, each and every edition. We never accept freebies for positive coverage, so you can rely on us to tell it like it is.

QuickStart Guide 7

Explore Kraków 21

Worth a Trip:

The Best of Kraków 121

Kraków's Best Walks

Kraków's Best ...

Survival Guide 143

QuickStart Guide

Welcome to Kraków

If you believe the legends, Kraków was founded on the defeat of a dragon, and it's true a mythical atmosphere permeates its medieval streets and squares. However, there's more to this royal, regal former capital than history and myth. The squares and alleyways pulse with modern life – creating a harmonious, infectious blend of past and present.

Kraków's main market square, Rynek Główny (p44)
CAPTURE/GETTY IMAGES ©

Kraków
Top Sights

Wawel Royal Castle (p24)

The centre of spiritual and political power in Poland for five centuries, these days it's a stirring symbol of an enduring – and surviving – Polish state. Centuries of Polish rulers are buried beneath the cathedral.

ANNA LURYE/GETTY IMAGES ©

Rynek Underground (p40)

This high-tech archaeological museum – situated three metres below the ground – tells the amazing 800-year-old story of the development of Kraków and its main market square.

IMAGE BY TOMASZ KALARUS, THE HISTORICAL MUSEUM OF THE CITY OF CRACOW

JAROSŁAW MORAWCIK SHUTTERSTOCK ®

St Mary's Basilica (p38)

A Gothic masterpiece of soaring proportions, Kraków's main church – and symbol of the city – dazzles with painted glass and an intricately carved altarpiece dating back more than 500 years.

Schindler's Factory (p84)

Housed in Oskar Schindler's former enamel factory, this interactive museum goes well beyond the film *Schindler's List* to tell the entire story of life in Kraków under the Nazi occupation during WWII.

Galicia Jewish Museum (p64)

This thoughtful gallery forges links from the present day to the region's Jewish past, through a series of highly moving contemporary photographs and engaging, instructive text.

Auschwitz-Birkenau Memorial & Museum (p114)

An essential excursion to the most notorious of the German Nazi extermination camps that operated during WWII. It's certainly an emotionally trying trip, but a necessary and rewarding one as well.

Wieliczka Salt Mine (p118)

Underground cathedrals, lakes and vast chambers – all hewn by man and all made from salt. It's much more interesting than it sounds and a great day out for the kids as well.

JÜRGEN RITTERBACH/GETTY IMAGES ©

ROXANA BASHYROVA/SHUTTERSTOCK ©

Collegium Maius (p42)

The oldest university building in the country holds unexpected charms, such as the scientific instruments used by former student Nicolaus Copernicus and the first known globe to mark out the American continent.

Kraków Local Life

Insider tips to help you find the real city

You've toured the Jewish Quarter in a golf cart and had coffee on the main market square – now it's time to lift the cover on tourist Kraków and see how the people who live here spend their time and have their fun.

The Old Town's Historic Clubs & Cafes (p44)

▶ Epic clubs
▶ Hidden restaurants

Kraków's main square, the Rynek Główny, is packed with tourists, and many locals, regrettably, keep their distance. But the square has always been the city's nerve centre and intellectual heart. Visit places where you can feel that old vibe.

Gallery Hopping in Kazimierz (p66)

▶ Cutting-edge design
▶ High-end art

Kazimierz is not only the city's go-to spot for nightlife and cafes; locals know it's also great for hunting down quirky shops and one-of-a-kind galleries that go beyond the standard souvenir and amber stores.

Podgórze's Quirkier Side (p86)

▶ Ancient sites
▶ Forgotten stories

Podgórze might be the city's most interesting district, but its secrets go deeper than Schindler's Factory and the Jewish ghetto. Residents know this neighbourhood on the edge has more to offer travellers willing to wander off the beaten track.

Workers' Paradise in Nowa Huta (p112)

▶ Socialist-Realist architecture
▶ Communist history

Far from the medieval finery of the Rynek Główny, Nowa Huta was a communist-era attempt at a model workers' community. Part authoritarian, part utopian, it's worth the trip to admire the grandiose scale and harmonious futuristic architecture.

Arka Pana church in Nowa Huta (p113)

Cloth Hall (p48)

Other great places to experience the city like a local:

Food Trucks (p77)

Coffee Cargo (p91)

Las Wolski (p101)

Polskie Smaki (p54)

Polish Pizza (p74)

Milkbar Tomasza (p54)

BAL (p91)

Hala Targowa (p111)

Kraków
Day Planner

Day One

On your first day, get an early start to beat the crowds to the **Wawel Royal Castle** (p24). Spend the morning exploring the Royal Private Apartments and State Rooms and make your way to the **Wawel Cathedral** (p26). Take a break for lunch at **Miód Malina** (p31). Stop to admire the artistry in the **Basilica of St Francis** (p29) and to catch a glimpse of John Paul II waving from the **Papal Window** (p29).

From here, continue into the heart of the Old Town to the bustling Rynek Główny. See the square from above by climbing the **Town Hall Tower** (p48) and then from below at the **Rynek Underground** (p40). Listen to the *hejnał* (bugle call) on the hour from **St Mary's Basilica** (p38) and step inside to admire the church's dazzling interior.

Dine on French cuisine in a cellar at **Cyrano de Bergerac** (p53), or try something more contemporary at smart and trendy **Pino** (p52). Then get into the jazz at **Piec' Art** (p59) or **Harris Piano Jazz Bar** (p58).

Day Two

Spend your morning in Kazimierz, starting with coffee and bagels at **Bagelmama** (p77), followed by a visit to the excellent and moving **Galicia Jewish Museum** (p64). Stroll down ul Szeroka, stopping to pay your respects at the **Remuh Synagogue** (p70) and **Remuh Cemetery** (p71), or peruse the collection at the **Jewish Museum** (p70) in the Old Synagogue.

For lunch, in keeping with the Jewish theme, stop for hummus and grilled meats at **Hamsa** (p74). For Polish fare, sample some *pierogi* (dumplings) at **Pierogi Mr Vincent** (p77). In the afternoon, wander across the river to Podgórze to Plac Bohaterów Getta, the centre of the Nazi wartime Jewish ghetto. Pop into the museum at the **Pharmacy Under the Eagle** (p89) and then walk over to **Schindler's Factory** (p84).

In the evening, try the excellent Polish food at **Sąsiedzi** (p74) and then stroll busy Plac Nowy for drinks and fun after. Some cafes and bars we love here include **Singer Cafe** (p78), **Mleczarnia** (p78) and **Alchemia** (p78). **Bar Atelier** (p78) has a hidden garden if you catch a warm evening.

Short on time?
We've arranged Kraków's must-sees into these day-by-day itineraries to make sure you see the very best of the city in the time you have available.

Day Three

☀ You've touched on the main sights, so today is excursion day. The two most popular day trips are to catch the train to Oświęcim to the **Auschwitz-Birkenau Memorial & Museum** (p114) or grab a bus or train to the **Wieliczka Salt Mine** (p118). Don't try to visit both in one day – it's too taxing. Auschwitz-Birkenau is an all-day affair, with 90 minutes of travel time in each direction.

☀ If you've opted for Wieliczka and get an early start, that leaves the afternoon open. For lunch, try **Glonojad** (p108), conveniently located on Plac Matejki, near where the Wieliczka buses drop you. After lunch, spend the afternoon wandering the planned workers' community of **Nowa Huta** (p112) to admire the 1950s Socialist-Realist architecture.

🌙 After a long day, try something low-key for the evening. Book a table at **Trufla** (p52) for very good Italian. After dinner, walk across Art Nouveau–rich Plac Szczepański and stroll along the Planty, the parkland that surrounds the Old Town. Finish with drinks at **Cafe Bunkier** (p56).

Day Four

☀ Begin the day with coffee and pastry from **Charlotte Chleb i Wino** (p52) and walk over to the **Collegium Maius** (p42). Time your arrival for 9am or 11am to check out the mechanical, medieval puppet display in the courtyard before visiting the museum. Head west for one more museum: the Gallery of 20th-Century Polish Painting at the **National Museum** (p98).

☀ Make your way to **Dynia** (p101) for lunch. If it's raining, spend the afternoon browsing books at **Massolit Books & Café** (p103). If you find something good, hunker down at **Café Szafe** (p102) and wait out the weather. If it's sunny, take bus 134 from near the National Museum to Las Wolski, where you can visit the animals at the **Zoological Gardens** (p99) and climb to the sky on **Piłsudski Mound** (p98).

🌙 For dinner, we love the bistro-style food at **ZaKładka Food & Wine** (p90) in an up-and-coming part of Podgórze. After dinner, chill out at **Forum Przestrzenie** (p92), the coolest retro-fitted communist hotel (now drinks bar) you're ever likely to see.

Need to Know

**For more information,
see Survival Guide (p143)**

Currency
Polish złoty (zł)

Language
Polish

Visas
Generally not required for stays of up to three months.

Money
ATMs widely available and credit cards accepted at many restaurants and hotels across the city.

Mobile Phones
Phones use GSM 900/1800, compatible with mobile phones from the rest of Europe, Australia and New Zealand, but not with most North American phones.

Time
Central European Time (GMT/UTC plus one hour)

Plugs & Adapters
Plugs have two round pins; electric current is 230V, 50Hz. North American travellers will need adaptors and – depending on the device – transformers.

Tipping
In pubs, cafes and restaurants, add 10% if service has been good. Taxi drivers won't expect a tip, but it's fine to round up to the nearest 5zł to reward special service.

① Before You Go

Your Daily Budget

Budget less than €50
- ► Dorm beds €10–20
- ► Excellent supermarkets for self-catering
- ► Herring and a shot of vodka €3

Midrange €50–150
- ► Double room at midrange hotel €80–100
- ► Dinner with starter and wine €25–30
- ► Museum admission €5

Top End more than €150
- ► Double room at luxury hotel €100–180
- ► Four-course dinner at best restaurant €60
- ► Best seat at the opera €50

Useful Websites

Lonely Planet (www.lonelyplanet.com/krakow) Destination information, hotel bookings, traveller forum and more.

Magiczny Kraków (www.krakow.pl) Official tourism website.

Kraków Info (www.krakow-info.com) Great overview of practical tips.

Karnet Kraków (www.karnet.krakow.pl) Useful schedule of cultural events.

Advance Planning

Three months before Book your hotel room, especially if you're travelling over a holiday.

One month before Buy tickets online for Wawel Royal Castle and Rynek Underground. Check Karnet Kraków to see what's on.

One week before Buy tickets online for Schindler's Factory. Reserve tables at better restaurants.

2 Arriving in Kraków

Most visitors enter via the international airport, **John Paul II International Airport**, or the main train station, **Kraków Główny**. The **bus station** is adjacent to the train station and transport options are the same. Public transportation and taxis are available from all entry points.

✈ From John Paul II International Airport

Take a taxi, the train, or bus 292 or 208, to **Kraków Główny Train Station**, from where you can find onward transport.

🚊 From Kraków Główny Train Station (or Bus Station)

Destination	Best Transport
Old Town	Walk 10 minutes south, passing through Galeria Krakowska shopping centre and an underpass, to arrive at the northern end of Old Town.
Wawel Hill	Taxi or tram 10 to 'Wawel'
Kazimierz	Taxi or tram 3, 19, 24 to 'Miodowa' or tram 10 to 'Plac Wolnica'
Podgórze	Taxi or tram 3, 19, 24 to 'Plac Bohaterów Getta'

✈ At the Airport

John Paul II International Airport The international arrivals hall is well set up, with numerous ATMs in the concourse as well as restaurants and cafes, car-hire desks and a branch of the InfoKraków tourist information office (open daily 9am-7pm).

3 Getting Around

Kraków's public transport system is affordable and efficient. Most visitors will be able to get around easily by walking or hopping on a tram. Public buses run from the airport to the centre. Taxis fill the gap after 11pm when most trams and buses stop running.

🚊 Tram

In the centre, the network is dense, and you'll likely have several options for moving from place to place. Trams 1, 6, 8, 13 and 18 are best for reaching the Rynek Główny. Trams 6, 8 and 13 run from near the Rynek to Kazimierz. Trams 3, 9, 19, 24, 50 are best for Podgórze. Use the Plac Bohaterów Getta stop for Schindler's Factory.

🚌 Bus

Buses are aimed more at residents and serve commuters moving to and from outlying districts. Tickets for buses and trams are interchangeable. Individual tickets allow for unlimited transfers between trams and buses. Validate your ticket on boarding the vehicle.

🚗 Taxis

Taxis are convenient for late-night rides back to the hotel and airport transfers. The number of rogue drivers has decreased in recent years, but it's safer to order a taxi by phone than hail one from the street.

🚲 Bicycle

There are too many cars and trams sharing the roads to call Kraków a cycling paradise. That said, officials continue to build out the trail infrastructure and there are some beautiful rides along the banks of the Vistula.

Kraków
Neighbourhoods

Worth a Trip

◉ Top Sights

Auschwitz-Birkenau
Memorial & Museum

Wieliczka Salt Mine

Old Town (p36)

The centre of Kraków life
since the 13th century,
and still going strong.
Packed with historical
buildings, monuments
and much more.

◉ Top Sights

St Mary's Basilica

Rynek Underground

Collegium Maius

Wawel Hill & Around (p22)

The hill-top castle was
the seat of kings for over
500 years, from the
earliest days of the
Polish state.

◉ Top Sights

Wawel Royal Castle

Western Kraków (p94)

This mainly residential
area with large wooded
areas and historic
mounds represents
Kraków at its most
artistic and verdant.

Podgórze (p82)

A working class district
on the upswing as
clubs and cafes open
up and trendy
Kazimierz spills over
across the river.

◉ Top Sights

Schindler's Factory

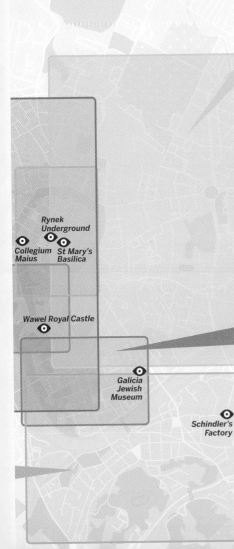

Eastern Kraków (p104)
Here Kraków loses its aura of medieval magic and holiday haven and takes on the rhythms of the workaday world.

Rynek Underground

Collegium Maius

St Mary's Basilica

Wawel Royal Castle

Kazimierz (p62)
Once an independent town, its mixed Jewish and Christian populations created a pair of distinctive communities side by side.

⊙ Top Sights
Galicia Jewish Museum

Galicia Jewish Museum

Schindler's Factory

Explore
Kraków

Worth a Trip

Kraków's city skyline
HENRYK T. KAISER/GETTY IMAGES ©

Explore

Wawel Hill & Around

The symbol of a nation, Wawel Hill is the silent guardian of a millennium of Polish history. The hilltop castle was the seat of kings and queens from the earliest days of the Polish state, and the site of the most solemn ceremonies and celebrated moments. Many Polish monarchs found their final resting place beneath Wawel Cathedral (pictured).

HENRYK T. KAISER/GETTY IMAGES ©

The Sights in a Day

It's **Wawel Royal Castle** (p24) day, so hit the morning running. Hopefully, you've pre-booked a morning tour of either the castle's **State Rooms** or **Royal Private Apartments**. After the tour, peek in at **Wawel Cathedral** (p26) and be sure to head downstairs to the crypts to see a long parade of tombs and stone caskets holding the remains of Polish luminaries across the ages.

Leave the castle grounds through the **Dragon's Den** (p26) and then wend your way back toward ul Grodzka for lunch. For something simple but good try the traditional Polish milk bar **Bar Grodzki** (p32). For the rest of the afternoon, check out the Art Nouveau stained glass at the **Basilica of St Francis** (p29) and the Baroque statuary outside the **Church of SS Peter & Paul** (p31).

Cap off the day with a splurge-worthy Polish meal in a Gothic cellar at **Pod Aniołami** (p32). If it's summer and you'd rather dine al fresco, try for a garden table at **La Campana Trattoria** (p32). For entertainment, check out either the Church of SS Peter & Paul or the nearby **Church of St Giles** (p35) to see if there's a concert on. **Prozak 2.0** (p34) is one of the city's leading outlets for electronic dance music and general revelry.

Top Sights
Wawel Royal Castle (p24)

Best of Kraków
Food
Bar Grodzki (p32)

Drinking & Nightlife
Prozak 2.0 (p34)

Historical Sites
Wawel Royal Castle (p24)
Wawel Cathedral (p26)
Basilica of St Francis (p29)

Architecture
Church of SS Peter & Paul (p31)

With Kids
Dragon's Den (p26)

Shopping
Kobalt (p35)
Amber (p35)
Boruni Gallery (p35)

Getting There
🚋 **Trams** 6, 8, 10, 13 and 18 drop you at the foot of Wawel Castle.

🚋 **Trams** 1, 6, 8, 13 and 18 bisect the Old Town along Plac Dominikański and are good for reaching attractions along ul Grodzka.

Top Sights
Wawel Royal Castle

Any trip to Kraków inevitably involves a trek up stately Wawel Hill to pay respects to the former seat of the Polish monarchy. Even if you don't plan on entering any of the paid attractions, it's definitely worth the effort. The grounds are free to enter, and the scale, architecture and exuberant atmosphere – usually infused with the boisterous laughter of school kids on a field trip – are impressive. The way to Wawel begins at the southern end of ul Kanonicza, from where a lane leads uphill, past the equestrian statue of Tadeusz Kościuszko, and into a vast open central square.

👁 Map p28, C4

☎ 12 422 5155

www.wawel.krakow.pl

Zamek Królewski na Wawelu

Wawel Hill

⊙ grounds 6am-dusk

🚌 6, 8, 10, 13, 18

Don't Miss

State Rooms

The largest and most impressive exhibition at Wawel Castle are these 20 or so **chambers** (🖉Wawel Visitor Centre 12 422 5155; www.wawel.krakow.pl; adult/concession 18/11zł; 🕓9.30am-1pm Mon, to 5pm Tue & Fri, to 4pm Wed & Thu, 11am-6pm Sat & Sun; 🚌6, 8, 10, 13, 18) that have been restored to their original Renaissance and early-Baroque style and crammed with period furnishings and works of art. The **Hall of Senators** houses a magnificent series of 16th-century Arras tapestries following the story of Adam and Eve, Cain and Abel, or Noah (they are rotated periodically). The **Hall of Deputies** has a fantastic coffered ceiling with 30 individually carved and painted wooden heads.

Royal Private Apartments

A visit to the **Royal Private Apartments** (🖉Wawel Visitor Centre 12 422 5155; www.wawel.krakow.pl; adult/concession 25/19zł; 🕓9.30am-5pm Tue-Sun Apr-Oct, to 4pm Tue-Sat Nov-Mar; 🚌6, 8, 10, 13, 18) imparts great insight into how the other half (at least in the 16th century) once lived. You'll see plenty of magnificent old tapestries, mostly northern French and Flemish, hanging on the walls. Other highlights include the so-called Hen's Foot, female monarch Jadwiga's gemlike chapel in the northeast tower, and the sumptuous Gdańsk-made furniture in the Alchemy Room.

Crown Treasury & Armoury

The **treasury and armoury** (🖉Wawel Visitor Centre 12 422 5155; www.wawel.krakow.pl; adult/concession 18/11zł; 🕓9.30am-1pm Mon, to 5pm Tue-Sun Apr-Oct, to 4pm Tue-Sun Nov-Mar; 🚌6, 8, 10, 13, 18) are housed in vaulted Gothic rooms surviving from the 14th-century castle. The most famous object in the

☑ **Top Tips**

▸ Attractions at Wawel Royal Castle must be booked and paid for separately. Grounds admission is free.

▸ Don't feel you have to see everything to have 'done' the castle. Instead, pick one or two attractions and focus your visit on those.

▸ The **Wawel Visitor Centre** (🖉guides 12 422 1697, info 12 422 5155; www.wawel.krakow.pl; Wawel Hill; 🕓9am-6pm; 🚌6, 8, 10, 13, 18) can be a life-saver. The harried but polite staff here can help plan your visit and pre-book tours and tickets.

▸ Most of the attractions can only be seen by guided tour, which must be booked in advance.

✕ **Take a Break**

There's a cafe and restaurant within the **Wawel Visitor Centre**. For something good and not too far away from the entrance to the castle complex (and much better quality), try Miód Malina (p31).

treasury is the *Szczerbiec* ('Jagged Sword'), dating from the mid-13th century, which was used at all Polish coronations from 1320 onward. The armoury features a collection of old weapons from various epochs, including crossbows, swords, lances and halberds.

Lost Wawel

Located in the old royal kitchen, this **exhibition** (☑ Wawel Visitor Centre 12 422 5155; www.wawel.krakow.pl; adult/concession 10/7zł; ⏰9.30am-1pm Mon, to 5pm Tue-Sun Apr-Oct, to 4pm Tue-Sun Nov-Mar; 🚌6, 8, 10, 13, 18) features the very oldest treasures up here, including remnants of the late-10th-century Rotunda of SS Felix and Adauctus, reputedly the first church in Poland, as well as various archaeological finds and models of previous Wawel churches.

Wawel Cathedral

The **cathedral** (☑12 429 9515; www. katedra-wawelska.pl; Wawel 3; cathedral free, combined entry for crypts, bell tower & museum adult/concession 12/7zł; ⏰9am-5pm Mon-Sat, from 12.30pm Sun; 🚌6, 8, 10, 13, 18) has been the site of countless coronations, funerals and burials of Poland's monarchs and strongmen over the centuries – and is suitably decked out. Highlights include the Holy Cross Chapel, Sigismund Chapel, Sigismund Bell and the Royal Crypts. Touring all of these could take the whole afternoon, but try not to miss the crypts, where a 'who's who' of Polish royalty and power are buried.

Wawel Cathedral Museum

Diagonally opposite the cathedral is this **treasury** (☑12 429 9515; www. katedra-wawelska.pl; Wawel 3; adult/concession 12/7zł, ticket covers admission to Royal Crypt & Sigismund Bell; ⏰9am-5pm Mon-Sat; 🚌6, 8, 10, 13, 18) of historical and religious objects from the cathedral. There are plenty of exhibits, including church plates and royal funerary regalia, but not a single crown. They were all apparently stolen from the treasury by the Prussians in 1795 and reputedly melted down.

Dragons Den

If you've had enough of high art and Baroque furnishings, complete your Wawel trip with a visit to the cheesy **Dragon's Den** (Smocza Jama; www. wawel.krakow.pl; admission 3zł; ⏰10am-6pm Apr-Oct; 🚌6, 8, 10, 13, 18), former home of the legendary Wawel Dragon and an easy way to get down from Wawel Hill. The entrance to the cave is next to the Thieves' Tower (Baszta Złodziejska) at the southwestern end of the complex. From here you'll have a good panorama over the Vistula River and the suburbs further west.

Exhibition of Oriental Art

A collection of 17th-century Turkish banners and weaponry, captured after the Battle of Vienna and displayed along with a variety of old Persian carpets, Chinese and Japanese ceramics, and other Asian antiques.

Understand

The Seat of Polish Kings and Queens

The buildings on Wawel Hill, including the castle and cathedral, constitute the most significant architectural collection in Poland.

The Early Centuries

There's been a royal building here for the better part of 1000 years. The first significant structures date from the 11th century and were commissioned by King Bolesław I Chrobry. His relatively small residence was given a big Gothic makeover in the 14th century, though much of that castle burned down in 1499. Soon after, King Zygmunt I Stary (Sigismund I the Old; 1506–48) commissioned a new residence in the then-fashionable Renaissance style, and within 30 years the palace had been built. Despite further alterations, the three-storey structure, complete with a courtyard arcaded on three sides, has been preserved to this day.

No Longer Royal

Once the Polish capital was transferred to Warsaw at the end of the 16th century, the Wawel buildings lost something of their *raison d'être*, though coronations and celebrations continued to take place. The grounds were repeatedly sacked by marauding Swedish and Prussian armies in the 17th and 18th centuries, and the castle was occupied in the 19th century by the Austrians, who intended to make Wawel a barracks and move the royal tombs below the cathedral elsewhere. They never got that far, but they did turn the royal kitchen and coach house into a military hospital and raze two churches. They also built a new ring of massive brick walls, largely ruining the original Gothic fortifications.

Wawel after Independence

After Kraków was incorporated into the re-established Poland after WWI, Wawel became a residence of the Polish president. Restoration work was undertaken until the outbreak of WWII. During the war, Wawel again assumed its historic role as a seat of power, but this time far more reluctantly. Kraków became the capital of German-occupied Poland, with Wawel serving as the residence for Nazi Governor General Hans Frank. After the war, further restoration work began and the complex was transformed into its current function as a museum and repository of national memory.

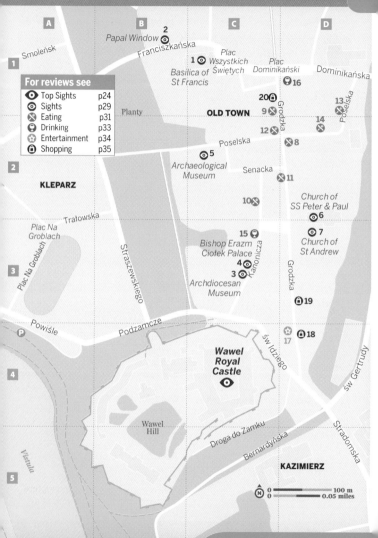

A

B

2
Papal Window ◉

C

Smoleńsk

Franciszkańska

1 ◉ Plac
Wszystkich
Basilica of Świętych
St Francis

Plac
Dominikański

Dominikańska

◉ 16

D

For reviews see

◉ Top Sights	p24
◉ Sights	p29
✕ Eating	p31
🍷 Drinking	p33
★ Entertainment	p34
🔒 Shopping	p35

Planty

OLD TOWN

20 🔒

9 ✕ Grodzka

13
✕ Poselska

14
◉

12 ◉

8 ✕

◉ 5

Poselska

Archaeological
Museum

Senacka

11 ✕

KLEPARZ

Trałowska

10 ✕

Church of
SS Peter & Paul
◉ 6

Plac Na
Groblach

Straszewskiego

15 🍷

◉ 7

Bishop Erazm
Ciołek Palace

4 ◉

Church of
St Andrew

Kanonicza

3 ◉

Grodzka

Plac Na Groblach

Archdiocesan
Museum

Powiśle

◉ 19

Podzamcze

🍷
17

🔒 18

**Wawel
Royal
Castle**
◉

św Idziego

św Gertrudy

Wawel
Hill

Vistula

Droga do Zamku

KAZIMIERZ

Stradomska

Bernardyńska

Ⓝ 0 ———————— 100 m
0 ———————— 0.05 miles

Archdiocesan Museum

Sights

Basilica of St Francis
CHURCH

1 ◎ Map p28, C1

Duck into the dark basilica on a sunny day to admire the artistry of Stanisław Wyspiański, who designed the fantastic Art Nouveau stained-glass windows. The multicoloured deity in the chancel above the organ loft is a masterpiece. From the transept, you can also enter the Gothic cloister of the Franciscan Monastery to admire the fragments of 15th-century frescoes. (Bazylika Św Franciszka; ☏ 12 422 5376; www.franciszkanska.pl; Plac Wszystkich Świętych 5; ⊙ 10am-4pm Mon-Sat, closed Sun during mass; ☏ 1, 6, 8, 13, 18)

Papal Window
MEMORIAL

2 ◎ Map p28, B1

When visiting Kraków, Pope John Paul II used to address his followers from this window of the Bishop's Palace, overlooking ul Franciszkańska. The area is filled with candles on important anniversaries, such as the former pope's birthday or anniversary of his death. These days, there's a photo of John Paul II in the window to keep his memory alive. (ul Franciszkańska 3; ⊙ Closed to the public; ☏ 1, 6, 8, 13, 18)

Archdiocesan Museum
MUSEUM

3 ◎ Map p28, C3

This collection of religious sculpture and paintings, dating from the 13th

Understand
'Smok' The Magic Dragon

Wawel Castle is home to the city's oldest legends, including at least one involving a fire-breathing dragon. Long ago, the story goes, during Prince Krak's reign, a nasty dragon lived in the cave below Wawel Hill, terrorising Kraków town. A fire-breathing menace, the scaly Smok ravaged residents and livestock, leaving death and destruction in his wake. His favourite food was beautiful young virgins.

Prince Krak feared for the life of his own daughter Wanda, and he offered her hand in marriage to any suitor who could slay the dragon. Many died trying. Finally, a poor young cobbler came up with a scheme to trick the dragon. He stuffed a sheep with sulphur and left the tasty morsel outside the dragon's lair. The dragon fell for it.

The dragon devoured the sheep, then retreated to the Vistula River to quench his unbearable thirst. He drained the river, causing his stomach to swell and inciting a massive explosion. The dragon was defeated! The cobbler was a hero! The virgins were safe! And Wanda and the cobbler lived happily ever after.

to 16th centuries, is located in a 14th-century townhouse. Also on display is the room where Karol Wojtyła (the late Pope John Paul II) lived from 1958 to 1967, complete with his furniture and belongings – including his skis. There's a treasury of gifts he received here, too. (Muzeum Archidiecezjalne; ☑12 421 8963; www.muzeumkra.diecezja.pl; ul Kanonicza 21; adult/concession 5/3zł; ◷10am-4pm Tue-Fri, to 3pm Sat & Sun; ◻6, 8, 10, 13, 18)

Bishop Erazm Ciołek Palace
MUSEUM

4 ◉ Map p28, C3

Quaint Kanonicza is the perfect street to put a palace and fill it with age-old paintings and sculpture. This newish branch of the National Museum contains two exhibits of religious artwork. The Art of Old Poland (12th to 18th centuries) includes loads of Gothic paintings, altar pieces and a room devoted to sculptor Veit Stoss. The second exhibit focuses on Orthodox art. (☑12 433 5920; www.mnk.pl; ul Kanonicza 17; adult/concession 12/7zł; ◷10am-6pm Tue-Sat, to 4pm Sun; ◻6, 8, 10, 13, 18)

Archaeological Museum
MUSEUM

5 ◉ Map p28, C2

You can learn about Małopolska's history from the Palaeolithic period up until the early Middle Ages here, but you'll be most enthralled by the collection of ancient Egyptian artefacts, including both human and animal mummies. There are also more than 4000 iron coins from the 9th century. The gardens are a lovely place for a stroll afterwards. (☏12 422 7100; www.ma.krakow.pl; ul Poselska 3; adult/concession 9/6zł, free Sun; ⊙9am-3pm Mon, Wed & Fri, 9am-6pm Tue & Thu, 11am-4pm Sun, closed Sat; ☐1, 6, 8, 13, 18)

Church of SS Peter & Paul

CHURCH

6 ◎ Map p28, D2

The Jesuits erected this church, the first Baroque building in Kraków, after they had been brought to the city in 1583 to do battle with supporters of the Reformation. Designed on the Latin cross layout and topped with a large sky-lit dome, the church has a refreshingly sober interior, apart from some fine stucco decoration on the vault. (☏12 350 6365; www.apostolowie.pl; ul Grodzka 52a; ⊙9am-5pm Tue-Sat, 1.30-5.30pm Sun; ☐6, 8, 10, 13, 18)

Church of St Andrew

CHURCH

7 ◎ Map p28, D3

Breathtakingly, this church is almost a thousand years old. Built towards the end of the 11th century, much of its austere Romanesque stone exterior has been preserved. As soon as you enter, though, you're in a totally different world; its small interior was subjected to a radical Baroque overhaul in the 18th century. (☏12 422 1612; ul Grodzka 54; ⊙8am-6pm Mon-Fri; ☐6, 8, 10, 13, 18)

Eating

Miód Malina

POLISH €€€

8 ✕ Map p28, D2

The charmingly named 'Honey Raspberry' serves Polish dishes in colourful surrounds. Grab a window seat and order the wild mushrooms in cream, and any of the duck or veal dishes. There's a variety of beef steaks on the menu as well. The grilled sheep's cheese appetiser, served with cranberry jelly, is a regional specialty. Reservations essential. (☏12 430 0411; www.miodmalina.pl; ul Grodzka 40; mains 30-70zł; ⊙noon-11pm; 🛜; ☐1, 6, 8, 13, 18)

LONELY PLANET IMAGES/GETTY IMAGES ©

Miód Malina

Pod Aniołami
POLISH €€€

 9 Map p28, C1

This is the quintessential Krakovian restaurant; its main dining room occupies a Gothic cellar from the 13th century. Heavy wood furniture, stone walls and fraying tapestries evoke the Middle Ages, as do the grilled meats cooked over a beech-wood fire. The wild-boar steak marinated in juniper berries comes highly recommended. (☎12 421 3999; www.podaniolami.pl; ul Grodzka 35; mains 40-70zł; ⏰1pm-midnight; 🔊; 🚌1, 6, 8, 13, 18)

Understand
Lady With An Ermine

Leonardo da Vinci's masterpiece, **The Lady with an Ermine** (☎12 422 5155; www.wawel.krakow.pl; Wawel Hill; adult/concession 10/8zł; ⏰9.30am-5pm Tue-Fri, 10am-5pm Sat & Sun; 🚌6, 8, 10, 13, 18) is on display at Wawel Castle for the foreseeable future, as the painting's permanent home, the **Czartoryski Museum** in the Old Town, is undergoing a multiyear renovation. Along with the *Mona Lisa*, the 'Lady' is one of only a handful of da Vinci portraits of women. The painting has had an interesting history. It was stolen from Kraków by the Nazis in WWII and was returned by the Americans after the war in 1946.

La Campana Trattoria
ITALIAN €€€

10 Map p28, C2

Not that Kraków needed another Italian restaurant, but this one boasts the city's most delightful, flower-filled courtyard setting. On a summer day, there is no better place to sip pinot grigio and munch on antipasti. (☎12 430 2232; www.lacampana.pl; ul Kanonicza 7; mains 30-54zł; ⏰noon-11pm; 🚌1, 6, 8, 13, 18)

Bar Grodzki
POLISH €

11 Map p28, D2

Delightful, family-run *bar mleczny* (milk bar), but a slight step up from the typical cafeteria setting. Line up at the steam table and choose your food. Highlights include a range of coleslaws, delicious fruit compote to drink, and classic Polish mains like stuffed cabbage rolls. (☎12 422 6807; www.grodzkibar.zaprasza.net; ul Grodzka 47; mains 10-20zł; ⏰9am-7pm Mon-Sat, 10am-7pm Sun; 🚌1, 6, 8, 13, 18)

Balaton
HUNGARIAN €€

12 Map p28, C2

The long-standing Balaton has gotten a spiffy renovation and the old shabby restaurant most people remember is long gone. These days, waiters serve up plates of chicken paprikas and bowls of goulash in a clean, spare space free from kitsch. It's a popular spot in the evening, so best to book in advance. (☎12 422 0469; www.balaton.krakow.pl; ul Grodzka 37; mains 19-40zł; ⏰noon-10pm; 🚌1, 6, 8, 13, 18)

Bona

Corse

CORSICAN €€€

13 Map p28, D1

This Corsican restaurant serves one of the more unusual cuisines available in Kraków. Its nautical decor, with white-canvas sail material hanging from the ceiling, feels upscale but comfortable, and the dishes – baked sea bream, veal with grapes, beef fondue – are well prepared. (☏12 421 6273; www.corserestaurant.pl; ul Poselska 24; mains 40-70zł; ☺1-11pm; ☜; ☐1, 6, 8, 13, 18)

Taco Mexicano

MEXICAN €€

14 Map p28, D2

If you hanker after something from 'south of the border' and Slovakian

bread dumplings are not what you had in mind, this cantina is for you. It's popular with locals and visitors alike, and serves fairly authentic enchiladas, burritos and tacos. There's also a tapas menu, with all dishes priced at 8zł. (☏12 421 5441; www.tacomexicano.pl; ul Poselska 20; mains 25-40zł; ☺noon-10pm; ☜; ☐1, 6, 8, 13, 18)

Drinking

Bona

CAFE

15 Map p28, C3

Pleasant combination of cafe and bookshop, with its bookshelves sandwiched between the indoor and outdoor seating. Great choice for a pit stop on the way from the Old Town to Wawel. Buy a book and sip a coffee with a view of the Church of SS Peter & Paul across the way. (☑12 430 5222; www.bonamedia.pl; ul Kanonicza 11; ⊗11am-8pm; 🛜; 🚊1, 6, 8, 13, 18)

Prozak 2.0 CLUB

16 🚇 Map p28, D1

A legend in its own time, this nightlife giant entices revellers into its labyrinth of passageways, nooks and crannies. It specialises in presenting international DJs. (☑733 704 650; Plac Dominikański 6; ⊗8pm-late; 🛜; 🚊1, 6, 8, 13, 18)

Entertainment

Church of SS Peter & Paul CONCERT VENUE

Evening concerts of Vivaldi, Bach, Chopin and Strauss are performed at the Church of SS Peter & Paul (see 6 ◉ Map p28, D2) four nights a week by the Cracow Chamber Orchestra of Saint Maurice. Buy tickets at the door before the concert or at any InfoKraków tourist information office. (☑695 574 526; ul Grodzka 52a; tickets adult/concession 60/40zł; ⊗8pm Wed, Fri, Sat, Sun; 🚊1, 6, 8, 13, 18)

JÖRG HACKEMANN/SHUTTERSTOCK ©

Church of St Giles

Understand
Vodka & Beer

The Polish national drink, vodka (*wódka*), is normally drunk as a shot, followed by a pickle. Clear vodka is not the only species of the spirit. Indeed, there is a whole spectrum of varieties of vodka, from sweet to extra dry. These include fruit-flavoured delights, pepper vodka, and the famous grass-flavoured *żubrówka*, or 'bison vodka'.

These days, Polish drinking habits are changing, with tastes turning to beer instead of (or in addition to) vodka. There are several brands of good, locally brewed Polish *piwo*, such as Żywiec, Tyskie, Okocim and Lech, as well as a growing number of microbreweries.

Church of St Giles CONCERT VENUE

17 ⭐ Map p28, D4

This tiny church hosts intimate, late-afternoon organ concerts, arias and Bach cello recitals (depending on the schedule). Buy tickets at the door just before the concert or at any InfoKraków tourist information office. (Kościół św Idziego; ☎ 695 574 526; ul Grodzka 67; tickets adult/concession 60/40zł; ⏰ 5pm Tue-Fri; 🚋 6, 8, 10, 13, 18)

Shopping
Kobalt CERAMICS

18 🔒 Map p28, D4

Sells eye-poppingly beautiful ceramic designs from the western Polish city of Bolesławiec. The dishes, plates and bowls are all hand-painted with a unique stamping and brush technique, and can be found in kitchens around the country. (☎ 798 380 431; www.kobalt.com.pl; Grodzka 62; ⏰ 10am-8pm; 🚋 6, 8, 10, 13, 18)

Boruni Gallery JEWELLERY

19 🔒 Map p28, D3

If you are curious to know more about amber, also known as 'Baltic gold', swing by this spacious gallery to watch the informative video about the various types of amber and its production processes. A word of caution: beware the hard sell. (☎ 12 428 5086; www.boruni.pl; ul Grodzka 60; ⏰ 9am-9pm Mon-Sat, to 8pm Sun; 🚋 6, 8, 10, 13, 18)

Amber JEWELLERY

20 🔒 Map p28, C1

As the name implies, this shop sells everything amber, including amber necklaces, earrings, brooches, and pendants. Though the space is small, the selection is large. Most settings are made of silver. (☎ 12 430 2042; www.sukiennice.krakow.pl; ul Grodzka 29; ⏰ 10am-7pm Mon-Fri, to 3pm Sat; 🚋 1, 6, 8, 13, 18)

Explore

Old Town

The centre of Kraków life since the Tatar invasions of the 13th century, and still going strong. The Old Town is filled with historical buildings and monuments, including several museums and many churches. It's also packed with restaurants, galleries and allegedly has more bars per square metre than anywhere else in Europe. Classified as a Unesco World Heritage site since 1978, it is largely car-free.

MILAN GONDA/SHUTTERSTOCK ©

The Sights in a Day

☼ Start your day with coffee and croissants at **Charlotte Chleb i Wino** (p52) and make your way to the **Cloth Hall** (p48). Hopefully, you've pre-booked a tour at the **Rynek Underground** (p40). If not, buy tickets for later in the day and spend the morning visiting **St Mary's Basilica** (p38) and taking in the square's carnival vibe. Art fans should see the **Gallery of 19th-Century Polish Painting** (p48); kids may want to climb the **Town Hall Tower** (p48).

☼ You're spoilt for choice with lunch on the main square. If authentically Polish is the main criteria, check out **U Babci Maliny** (p54), while for something more upscale, **Ed Red** (p52) features decently priced lunch specials. For the rest of the afternoon, visit the museum at the **Collegium Maius** (p42). Stroll the Planty and have afternoon drinks at **Cafe Bunkier** (p56).

☾ In nice weather reserve a garden table at **Trufla** (p52), or enjoy excellent French food at **Cyrano de Bergerac** (p53). For drinks, **Re** (p59) has a great beer garden, and if you'd like jazz with your beer, try **Harris Piano Jazz Bar** (p58). The Old Town is clubbing central. Hot clubs include **Frantic** (p58), while **Hush Live** (p57) offers a rare chance to experience the infectious cheesiness of a local brand of disco called 'Disco Polo'.

For a local's day in Old Town, see p44.

👁 Top Sights

St Mary's Basilica (p38)

Rynek Underground (p40)

Collegium Maius (p42)

🔍 Local Life

Historic Clubs & Cafes (p44)

♥ Best of Kraków

Food
Cyrano de Bergerac (p53)

Polskie Smaki (p54)

Trufla (p52)

U Babci Maliny (p54)

Drinking
Ambasada Śledzia (p56)

Black Gallery (p57)

Café Bunkier (p56)

Café Camelot (p56)

Hush Live (p57)

Getting There

🚊 **Trams** 1, 6, 8, 13 and 18 stop at Plac Dominikański, the closest tram to the Rynek Główny.

🚊 **Trams** 2, 4, 14, 19, 20 and 24 stop near the Florian Gate and serve the northern end of Old Town.

Top Sights
St Mary's Basilica

Overlooking the main square, this striking red-brick church, best known simply as St Mary's, is dominated by two towers of different heights. The first church here was built in the 1220s and following its destruction during a Tatar raid, construction of the basilica began. Tour the exquisite interior, with its remarkable carved wooden altarpiece, and in summer climb the tower for excellent views. Don't miss the hourly *hejnał* (bugle call) from the taller tower.

👁 Map p46, C5

📞 12 422 0737

www.mariacki.com

Plac Mariacki 5, Rynek Główny

adult/concession church 10/5zł, tower 15/10zł

🕐 11.30am-5.30pm Mon-Sat, 2-5.30pm Sun

🚋 1, 6, 8, 13, 18

Don't Miss

Wall Paintings

The first details you'll notice on entering the church are the elaborate and colourful wall paintings. Many of these paintings are the work of the 19th-century Polish master of Realism, Jan Matejko, and they harmonise beautifully with the medieval architecture and the intricacy of the high altar. Don't forget to look up: also noteworthy is the dazzling star-flecked blue ceiling.

Stained-Glass Windows

The chancel, the chamber that surrounds the main altar, is illuminated by a series of magnificent stained-glass windows dating from the late-14th century. On the opposite side of the church, above the organ loft, is a fine Art Nouveau stained-glass window by the early-modern masters Stanisław Wyspiański and Józef Mehoffer.

Carved Altarpiece

Measuring 13m high and 11m wide, the church's celebrated altarpiece is the country's largest and most important piece of medieval art. It took a decade for its maker, Veit Stoss, to complete the work before it was consecrated in 1489. Stoss carved the piece in lime wood, and after that it was painted and gilded. The main scene represents the Assumption of the Virgin surrounded by the Apostles.

Tower

Be sure to listen for the bugler's call on the hour. The melody is as old as the church itself and is associated with many of the city's legends (see boxed text, p51). If you'd like to see how the city looks from way up here, you can pay a separate admission to climb the 239 steps of the 82m-high tower (bring your own bugle).

S-F/SHUTTERSTOCK ©

☑ Top Tips

▶ The best place to hear the bugle call and to see the bugler in action is to stand in the small courtyard in front of the **Church of St Barbara**.

▶ Worshippers can enter for free through the main entrance on the southwestern side; tourists must enter through the side door to the southeast and pay an admission price.

▶ The altarpiece is opened daily at 11.50am and closed at 5.30pm, except for Saturday night when it's left open for the Sunday morning mass.

▶ Though the church is crammed with visitors, try to exercise some discretion for the sake of the people who are there to worship, not sightsee.

✕ Take a Break

Green Day (p55), just a couple blocks away behind the church, is great for a pick-me-up smoothie or cheap and healthy lunch.

Top Sights
Rynek Underground

This fascinating, high-tech attraction beneath the market square consists of an hour-long underground walk through medieval market stalls and other long-forgotten chambers. It's a kind of 'traditional archaeological museum meets modern-day interactive space', dedicated to telling the city's 1000-year history in a way that's interesting to visitors of all ages.

👁 Map p46, C5

📞 12 426 5060

www.podziemiarynku.com

Rynek Główny 1

adult/concession 19/16zł, Tue free

🕙 10am-8pm Mon, to 4pm Tue, to 10pm Wed-Sun

🚊 1, 6, 8, 13, 18

Don't Miss

Audiovisual Delights

From the video images projected onto rising smoke that you see as you enter the underground, to the holograms and videos on display in the various chambers, all the way to the documentary films (subtitled) on city life through the ages at the end of the trail, the advanced technology employed here to tell Kraków's long story is a big part of the exhibition itself.

Early Kraków Life

The first part of the exhibition is given over to depictions of everyday life in the 13th and 14th centuries, with features on trade, transport and construction. Look for authentic paving stones from the 14th century as well as rebuilt dwellings of various craftspeople and traders. For the kids, there's a puppet show, as well as a ghoulish re-creation of an 11th-century cemetery, along with some exposed skeletons (and lots of other stuff).

Model of the City

One of the highlights is an impressive scale model of the city in the 15th century at the height of its royal power, which shows the importance of the walls and the geographic relationship of the Old Town to Wawel Royal Castle. In a nod to Paris, the model is illuminated by a pyramid-shaped skylight that juts into the surface of the Rynek and can be seen from above the ground.

Archaeological Finds

Museum buffs won't be disappointed either, as much of the latter part of the exhibition route is dedicated to exploring various nooks and ruins discovered during recent archaeological digs. On display here are the various tools and artefacts used over the years to explore the city's main square.

☑ Top Tips

▸ Buy tickets at a special ticket office on the western side of the Cloth Hall (numbered Sukiennice 21).

▸ Note the electronic board at the office that shows tour times and the number of tickets available at each time.

▸ The actual entrance to the tunnels is on the opposite side of the Cloth Hall, on the northeastern end.

▸ Tuesdays are free, but you'll have to book well in advance since tickets are given out quickly.

✕ Take a Break

There's a cafe in the museum and the Rynek itself has tons of options. One of our favourites for coffee or a light meal, Noworolski (p45), is conveniently located in the Cloth Hall building, right next to the entrance to the Rynek Underground.

Top Sights
Collegium Maius

The Collegium Maius, built as part of the Kraków Academy (now the Jagiellonian University), is the oldest surviving university building in Poland, and one of the best examples of 15th-century Gothic architecture in the city. It has a magnificent arcaded courtyard (open from 7am to dusk) and a fascinating university museum.

👁 Map p46, A5

📞 12 663 1521

www.maius.uj.edu.pl

ul Jagiellońska 15

adult/concession 16/12zł

🕙 10am-2.20pm Mon-Fri, to 1.20pm Sat

🚋 2, 13, 18, 20

Don't Miss

Courtyard Clock

Even if you're not visiting the interior, it's worth peeking in on the picturesque, late-Gothic courtyard that dates from the 15th century. Be sure to time your visit to arrive at an odd hour between 9am and 5pm to see a short 16th-century spectacle of music and wooden figures that pop out through the windows below the courtyard clock.

Copernicus' Instruments

The tour passes through several historic interiors, with the most interesting being the displays of 15th- and 16th-century scientific equipment, including globes and telescopes of the kind that would have been used by one of the university's best-known alumni, Nicolaus Copernicus, who studied here in the 1490s. Also on display are some of Copernicus' manuscripts.

Jagiellonian Globe

There are plenty of paintings, sculptures, drawings and decorative arts on display – as well as a separate exhibition given over to medieval painting and visual arts. For most visitors the highlight of all of these curios will be the Jagiellonian Globe (dating from around 1510), which is the oldest known surviving globe to depict the American continent.

Aula

The original Renaissance ceiling here is crammed with portraits of kings, benefactors and rectors of the university (five of whom were sent off by the Germans to Sachsenhausen concentration camp in 1939). The treasury contains everything from copies of the 1364 university foundation papers and Jan III Sobieski's hammered silver table, to an Oscar given to director Andrzej Wajda.

☑ Top Tips

▶ Visit is by guided tour only; tours begin every half hour.

▶ Throughout the year there are at least a couple of daily tours in English, normally held at 11am and 1pm.

▶ In summer it's advisable to reserve in advance, either in person or by phone.

▶ The courtyard can be entered free of charge.

▶ Try to visit at odd hours between 9am and 5pm (9am, 11am, 1pm, 3pm, 5pm, and 11am, 1pm, 3pm in winter time) when the replica clock on the south side chimes and its cast of characters go through their paces.

✕ Take a Break

There's a cafe inside the museum. If you're looking for something more substantial, **The Dorsz Pub & Restaurant** (☑12 422 2191; www.dorszfishand chips.pl; ul Św Anny 4; fish & chips large/small 26/17zł, mains 25-35zł; ◷noon-10pm; ☏; ☐2, 13, 18, 20) claims to be the city's only authentic fish and chips joint.

Local Life
Historic Clubs & Cafes

Kraków's main square, the Rynek Główny, is one of Central Europe's liveliest public arenas, filled with horse carriages, buskers, hawkers, and hundreds if not thousands of people sitting down to a cup of coffee and piece of cream cake. For centuries, this was not a tourist attraction but the city's nerve centre and intellectual heart. While much of the modern-day square has been given over to visitors, the following institutions are still going strong.

① Epic Club

Legendary **Klub Pod Jaszczurami** (🕿12 429 4538; www.podjaszczurami.pl; Rynek Główny 8; ⏱noon-1am Sun-Wed, to 3am Thu-Sat; 🚊1, 6, 8, 13, 18) has been packing in students for happenings since the 1960s, and the black-and-white photos of performances through the years plastered on the walls testify to its pedigree. It's suffered a bit of a climbdown these days, hosting karaoke nights and DJs, but peek inside and

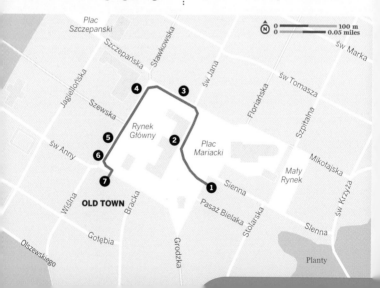

see the main stage, which still crackles with that old vibe.

❷ Political Favourite

Even if you don't stop for a coffee at **Noworolski** (📞 515 100 998, 12 422 4771; www.noworolski.com.pl; Rynek Główny 1, Sukiennice; ⊗ 8.30am-midnight; 🚊 1, 6, 8, 13, 18), pause to admire the stunning Art Nouveau interiors by Polish artist Józef Mehoffer. As the sign outside says, the Noworolski has been here since 1910, serving the likes of Lenin and later becoming a favourite haunt of occupying German Nazi officers. It sailed through the communist period intact, and still feels timeless.

❸ Communist Classic

Clubs in Kraków come and go with the season, but **Feniks** (📞 12 421 5093; feniksklub.com; ul Św Jana 2; ⊗ 4pm-9.30pm Sun-Thu, to 5am Sat & Sun; 🛜; 🚊 1, 6, 8, 13, 18), hiding in plain sight right on the main square, is still largely unchanged from communist days. The red velvet curtains and white tablecloths lend a throwback feel.

❹ Flapper Style

Sure, the Polish food here at **Europejska** (📞 12 429 3493; www.europejska.pl; Rynek Główny 35; mains 25-45zł; ⊗ 8am-midnight; 🚊 2, 4, 14, 18, 20, 24) is good, but most people come to soak up the old-world atmosphere of the restaurant's two back rooms. Striped wallpaper, green-velvet banquettes and old gramophones lend a genuine 1920s, flapper-era feel.

❺ Rogues' Gallery

Vis-à-vis (📞 12 422 6961; Rynek Główny 29; ⊗ 8am-1am; 🚊 1, 6, 8, 13, 18), with its tiny stand-up bar, is famous for having the cheapest beer prices on the main square and for being a haunt of artists, painters, poets, singers and actors.

❻ Pub for the Ages

The **Piwnica Pod Baranami** (📞 12 422 0177; www.piwnicapodbaranami.krakow. pl; Rynek Główny 27; 🚊 1, 6, 8, 13, 18), or 'Under the Rams', harks back to the mid-1950s when it functioned as a 'literary cabaret'. Nowadays, the program is a bit sporadic, but the place continues to host a summer jazz festival in July and other concerts and recitals throughout the year. It's a classic Kraków cellar pub.

❼ Real Cakes & Apple Strudel

Sure, there are plenty of bigger and more attractive cafes than **Arlekin** (📞 12 430 2457; www.arlekin-krakow.pl; Rynek Główny 24; 🚊 2, 13, 18, 20) on the main square, but locals – particularly older Krakovian ladies of the blue-haired bent – still consider this small, narrow space to serve the best and most authentic cakes and pastries in town.

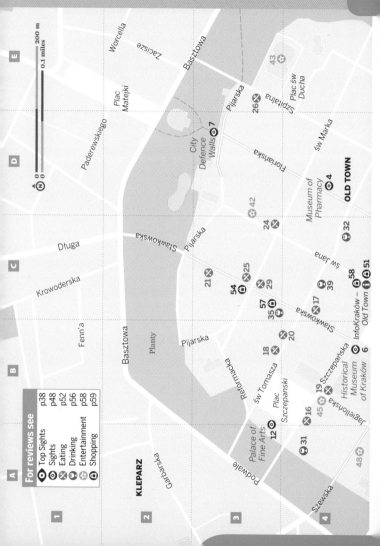

KLEPARZ

OLD TOWN

Worcella

Zacisze

Basztowa

Paderewskiego

Plac Matejki

Długa

Krowoderska

Fenn'a

Garbarska

Basztowa

Planty

Pijarska

Sławkowska

Reformacka

sw Tomasza

Plac Szczepanski

Podwale

Szewska

City Defence Walls ◆ 7

Pijarska

Florińska

sw Marka

Plac św Ducha

Szpitalna

Museum of Pharmacy ◎ 4

❼ 32

sw Jana

✪ 42

✕ 24

✕ 21

◎ 25

◎ 54

✕ 29

✕ 57

◎ 35

✕ 17

Sławkowska

✕ 20

✕ 18

✕ 19

Szczepańska

◎ 45

✕ 16

◎ 12

✕ 31

✪ 48

Jagiellońska

InfoKraków – Old Town ◎ 6

❼ 39

◆ 58

🏠 51

Historical Museum of Kraków

Palace of Fine Arts

🔵 26

🔵 43

0 200 m
0 0.1 miles

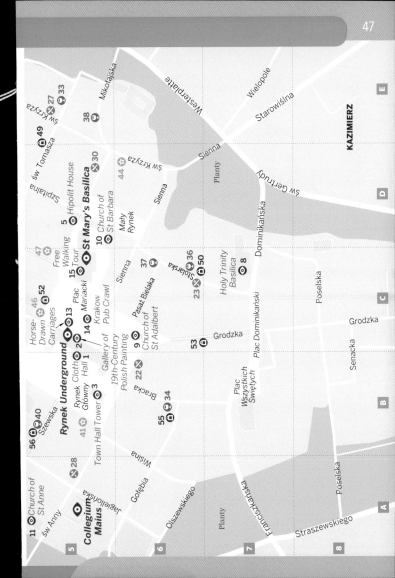

Sights

Cloth Hall
HISTORIC BUILDING

1 ◉ Map p46, B5

Dominating the middle of Rynek Główny, this building was once the centre of Kraków's medieval clothing trade. Created in the early 14th century when a roof was put over two rows of stalls, it was extended into a 108m-long Gothic structure, then rebuilt in Renaissance style after a 1555 fire; the arcades were a late-19th-century addition. The ground floor is now a busy trading centre for crafts and souvenirs; the upper floor houses the recently renovated **Gallery of 19th-Century Polish Painting**. (Sukiennice; www.museum.krakow.pl; Rynek Główny 1/3; admission free; 🚊1, 6, 8, 13, 18)

Gallery of 19th-Century Polish Painting
ART GALLERY

2 ◉ Map p46, C5

This gallery is separated into four separate rooms, each focusing on an important element of Polish art from the end of the 18th century up to WWI. The Chełmoński room is considered the strongest, focusing on Polish trends like Realism, Impressionism and Symbolist painting. (📞12 433 5400; www.mnk.pl; Rynek Główny 1; adult/concession 14/8zł, Sun free; 🕙10am-6pm Tue-Sun; 🚊1, 6, 8, 13, 18)

Town Hall Tower
TOWER

3 ◉ Map p46, B5

Southwest of the Cloth Hall, this soaring tower is all that is left of the 15th-century town hall which was dismantled in the 1820s. The 70m-tall tower can be climbed in the warmer months. (Wieża Ratuszowa; Rynek Główny 1; adult/concession 7/5zł; 🕙10.30am-6pm Apr-Oct; 🚊1, 6, 8, 13, 18)

Museum of Pharmacy
MUSEUM

4 ◉ Map p46, D4

The name of this museum doesn't sound that exciting, but the Jagiellonian University Medical School's Museum of Pharmacy is one of the largest museums of its kind in Europe and arguably the best. Accommodated in a beautiful historic townhouse, which is alone worth the visit, it features a 22,000-piece collection, including old laboratory equipment, rare pharmaceutical instruments, heaps of glassware, stoneware, mortars, jars, barrels, medical books and documents. (Muzeum Farmacj; 📞12 421 9279; www.muzeumfarmacji.pl; ul Floriańska 25; adult/concession 9/6zł; 🕙noon-6.30pm Tue, 10am-2.30pm Wed-Sun; 🚊2, 4, 14, 19, 20, 24)

Hipolit House
MUSEUM

5 ◉ Map p46, D5

Next to St Mary's Basilica, this branch of the Kraków City History Museum contains faithful recreations of townhouse interiors from the 17th to early 19th centuries. (Kamienica Hipolitów; 📞12 422 4219; www.mhk.pl; Plac Mariacki 3; adult/concession 9/7zł, free Wed; 🕙10am-5.30pm Wed-Sun; 🚊3, 10, 19, 24, 52)

Cloth Hall

Historical Museum of Kraków
MUSEUM

6 🎯 Map p46, B4

At the northern corner of the square, the collection within the 17th-century Krzysztofory Palace is home to *Cyberteka,* an interactive exhibition which charts the city from the earliest days to WWI. The museum features a bit of everything related to the city's past, including old clocks, armour, paintings, Kraków's celebrated *szopki* (nativity scenes), and the costume of the Lajkonik. (📞12 619 2335; www.mhk.pl; Rynek Główny 35; adult/concession 12/8zł, free Sat; ⏱10am-5.30pm Tue-Sun; 🚊2, 4, 14, 19, 20, 24)

City Defence Walls
HISTORIC SITE

7 🎯 Map p46, D3

This small museum includes entry to both the **Florian Gate** (Brama Floriańska) and the **Barbican** (Barbakan), among the few surviving remnants of the city's medieval defence walls. The Florian Gate was once the city's main entrance and dates from the 14th century. The Barbican, a circular bastion adorned with seven turrets, was built at the turn of the 16th century to lend additional protection. It was once connected to the gate by a narrow passage running over a moat. (Mury Obronne; 📞12 421 1361; www.mhk.pl; ul Pijarska; adult/concession 8/6zł; ⏱10.30am-6pm May-Oct; 🚊2, 4, 14, 19, 20, 24)

Holy Trinity Basilica   MONASTERY

8 ⊙ Map p46, C7

Originally built in the 13th century, this massive church was badly damaged by fire in 1850. Note the original 14th-century doorway at the main (western) entrance to the church. The monastery, just behind the northern wall of the church, is accessible from the street (enter an unmarked door at Stolarska 12). (Dominican Church; ☏12 423 1613; www.krakow.dominikanie.pl; ul Stolarska 12; ⊙9.30am-11.30am & 1.30pm-4.30pm, closed Sun during mass; ☐1, 6, 8, 13, 18)

Church of St Adalbert   CHURCH

9 ⊙ Map p46, C6

In the southern corner of the square is this small domed building. It's one of the oldest churches in the Old Town, dating from the 11th century. The original foundations of the building are located two metres below the surface. The church was closed to the public at the time of research and it wasn't clear when it would reopen. (Kościół Św Wojciecha; ☏12 422 8352; Plac Mariacki; ☐1, 6, 8, 13, 18)

Church of St Barbara   CHURCH

10 ⊙ Map p46, D5

South of St Mary's is this sombre 14th-century church sited on the small, charming Plac Mariacki, which until the early 19th century was a church-yard. St Barbara's was the cemetery chapel and served the Polish faithful during the Middle Ages (St Mary's was for Germans). Note the skull and crossbones on the north exterior; just inside the entrance is an open chapel featuring stone sculptures of Christ and three of the Apostles, attributed to the Stoss school. (Kościół Św Barbary; ☏12 428 1500; www.swietabarbara.jezuici.pl; Plac Mariacki; ⊙8am-6pm; ☐1, 6, 8, 13, 18)

Church of St Anne   CHURCH

11 ⊙ Map p46, A5

Designed by Tylman van Gameren and built in the late-17th century as a university church, the Church of St Anne was long the site of inaugurations of the academic year, doctoral promotions and a resting place for many university professors and rectors. A spacious, stark-white interior fitted out with fine furnishings, gravestones and epitaphs, and embellished with superb stuccowork and murals – all stylistically homogeneous – puts the church among the best classical Baroque buildings in Poland. (Kościół Św Anny; ☏12 422 5318; www.kolegiata-anna.pl; ul Św Anny 11; ⊙8am-6pm; ☐2, 13, 18, 20)

Palace of Fine Arts   GALLERY

12 ⊙ Map p46, B3

The centrepiece of the Art Nouveau Plac Szczepański is this elaborate edifice on its west side. An incredible frieze circles the building (product of Jacek Malczewski), while the busts on the facade honour Polish artists. The building is used for temporary art exhibits. (Pałac Sztuki; ☏12 422 6616; www.palac-sztuki.krakow.pl; Plac Szczepański 4; adult/concession 10/5zł; ⊙8.15am-6pm Mon-Fri, 10am-6pm Sat & Sun; ☐2, 4, 14, 18, 20, 24)

Horse-Drawn Carriages CARRIAGE

13 ⊙ Map p46, C5

The most romantic way to tour Kraków is by the horse-drawn carriages that line up at the northern end of Rynek Główny. You decide which route you want to take, or leave it up to the driver to take you for a trot round the sights of the Old Town or even down to Kazimierz. Negotiate the price in advance. (Rynek Główny; half/full hour 150/250zł; 🚍1, 6, 8, 13, 18)

Krakow Pub Crawl WALKING TOUR

14 ⊙ Map p46, C5

The tour visits four venues and includes unlimited drinks for an hour at the first bar. Meets nightly (9pm May-Oct) on the Rynek Główny (in front of the Adam Mickiewicz Statue). Book in advance over the website or simply show up for the tour. (www. krawlthroughkrakow.com; Rynek Główny; 60zł; ⊗9pm May-Oct; 🚍1, 6, 8, 13, 18)

Free Walking Tour WALKING TOUR

15 ⊙ Map p46, C5

These free walking tours of the Old Town and Kazimierz are provided by licensed tour guides who make their money from tips. Tours depart daily (May to October) at 10am and 3.30pm from in front of St Mary's Basilica on the Rynek Główny. Look for the tour guide holding the sign 'Free Walking Tour'. (🔗513 875 815; www.freewalkingtour. com; 🚍1, 6, 8, 13, 18)

Understand
The Trumpeter of Kraków

Every hour on the hour, a bugler plays a haunting melody from the steeple of the Basilica of St Mary's. The *hejnał* is a simple five-note tune that dates back as far as the church. It is played four times, once in each direction, and was perhaps a signal of the opening and closing of the city gates. Some sources claim the bugle calls were also used to warn of fires and sound other alarms. The tune ends oddly and abruptly, its final note cut off without conclusion. Nobody knows why, but it has given rise to an intriguing legend.

The story goes that the bugler played the *hejnał* to warn of an attack by marauding Mongols back in the 13th century. As he sounded the alarm, he was shot, his heart pierced with an arrow and his warning cut short. Alas, it is only a legend. Indeed, some claim the source of this story was an American writer, Eric Kelly, who described the tale in his 1929 children's book *The Trumpeter of Kraków*. Never mind – Krakovians have embraced this tradition with gusto. Nowadays, a team of several trumpeters is responsible for playing the *hejnał* every hour on the hour, around the clock. It is broadcast on Polish Radio daily at noon.

Eating

Charlotte Chleb i Wino BAKERY €€

16 Map p46, B4

This is the Kraków branch of a popular Warsaw restaurant serving croissants, French breads, salads and sandwiches. The crowd on artsy Plac Szczepański is suitably stylish as they tuck into their croque monsieurs and sip from excellent but affordable French wines. The perfect stop for morning coffee. (📞600 807 880; www.bistrocharlotte.pl; Plac Szczepański 2; salads & sandwiches 10-20zł; 🕓7am-midnight Mon-Thu, to 1am Fri & Sat, 9am-10pm Sun; 🛜; 🚊2, 4, 14, 18, 20, 24)

Ed Red STEAK €€€

17 Map p46, C4

This is a solid splurge option for the steaks – cuts include New York strip, ribeye and T-bone – made from dry-aged beef and using only local producers. Other mains include beef cheeks served on buckwheat, wild boar and free-range chicken. The interior, with walls painted in muted blues and browns, is straight out of a magazine. (📞690 900 555; www.edred.pl; ul Sławkowska 3; mains 35-60zł; 🕓7am-11pm; 🛜; 🚊2, 4, 14, 19, 20, 24)

Trufla ITALIAN €€

18 Map p46, B3

Affordable yet quality Italian food, including steaks, seafood, pasta and risotto – but no pizza. The decor is uncluttered: think hardwood floors and simple, wooden tables. Yet the overall ambience is relaxing. In summer, there's a pretty garden out back (to access the garden, walk through a corridor to the left of the main entrance). (📞12 422 1641; www.truflakrakow.pl; ul Św Tomasza 2; mains 22-35zł; 🕓9am-11pm Mon-Fri, 10am-11pm Sat & Sun; 🛜; 🚊2, 4, 14, 18, 20, 24)

Pino INTERNATIONAL €€

19 Map p46, B4

This airy space opened in 2015 and immediately drew crowds both for the playfully stylish interior of exposed brink and metal chairs splashed in mid-century pastels, and the inventive, eclectic menu ranging from sous-vide duck to steak tartare, as well as pizzas and burgers. (📞12 397 8045, 609 015 016; www.restauracjapino.pl; Plac Szczepański 4; mains 20-40zł; 🕓11am-11pm; 🛜; 🚊2, 4, 14, 18, 20, 24)

Del Papa ITALIAN €€

20 Map p46, B4

Traditional, upscale Italian food, including classics like beef and fish carpaccio, minestrone, thin-crust pizza and several pasta dishes. The menu holds a few less-traditional surprises, such as on our visit the grilled turkey served with shrimp and lavender on a bed of black rice. Mussels are prepared on Thursdays. The interior is refined but not stuffy. (📞12 421 8343; www.delpapa.pl; ul Św. Tomasza 6; mains 30-45zł; 🕓11.30am-11pm; 🛜; 🚊2, 4, 14, 18, 20, 24)

Cyrano de Bergerac

Cyrano de Bergerac FRENCH €€€

21 Map p46, C3

One of Kraków's top eateries, this restaurant serves fine, authentic French cuisine in one of the most beautiful cellars in the city. Artwork and tapestries add to the romance and in warmer months there's seating in a covered courtyard. (🖉12 411 7288; www. cyranodebergerac.pl; ul Sławkowska 26; mains 50-90zł; ⏰noon-11pm; 🚊2, 4, 14, 19, 20, 24)

Wentzl FRENCH, POLISH €€€

22 Map p46, B6

This historic eatery, dating back to 1792, is perched above the Rynek, with timbered ceilings, Oriental carpets and fine oil paintings all around. The food is sublime – cognac-flavoured foie gras, duck fillet glazed with honey, Baltic cod served with lentils and spinach – and the service is of a high standard. (🖉12 429 5299; www. restauracjawentzl.com.pl; Rynek Główny 21; mains 60-80zł; ⏰1-11pm; 🚊1, 6, 8, 13, 18)

Pimiento ARGENTINIAN €€€

23 Map p46, C6

This upmarket grill serves a dizzying array of steaks to suit both appetite and budget, and offers some reasonable vegetarian alternatives for the meat-averse. Factor the South American wine list into your calculations, and you have a classy night out. (🖉12 422 6672; www.pimiento.pl; ul Stolarska 13; mains 50-80zł; 🛜; 🚊1, 6, 8, 13, 18)

Local Life
Milk Bars

Milk bars (*bar mleczny*) were designed as cheap, no-frills cafeterias, subsidised by the state during the communist era in order to provide simple, wholesome meals for the poorest citizens. Several have survived into the modern day and are great for cheap, filling Polish food. **Milkbar Tomasza** (Map p46, D5; ☎12 422 1706; ul Św Tomasza 24; mains 10-18zł; ⏰8am-10pm Mon-Sat, 9am-10pm Sun; 🖥; 🚋3, 10, 19, 24, 52) is a modern take on the theme, where the paninis sit proudly beside the *pierogi* (dumplings). **Polskie Smaki** (Map p46, B4; ☎12 429 3869; www. polskie-smaki.pl; ul Św Tomasza 5; mains 10-20zł; ⏰8am-11pm; 🚋2, 4, 14, 18, 20, 24) borders on elegant, thanks to the vaulted ceiling, but the food is straightforward. Our favourites include stuffed peppers, pork cutlets and fried liver with mushrooms.

Farina   SEAFOOD €€€

24 🍴 Map p46, C3

We don't often advise ordering seafood so far inland, but let Farina be the exception to that rule. Your server will bring over a cart showing off the creatures that are flown in from the coast, not to mention fresh flaky pike-perch from local rivers. Also on offer: homemade pasta and more traditional Polish fare. (☎12 422 1680; www.farina.com.pl; ul Św Marka 16; mains 40-60zł; ⏰noon-11pm; 🖥; 🚋2, 4, 14, 19, 20, 24)

U Babci Maliny   POLISH €

25 🍴 Map p46, C3

This rustic basement restaurant is partly hidden in a courtyard. Simply descend the stairs like you know where you're going and follow your nose toward the dumplings, meat dishes and salads. One of the specialities, definitely worth a try, is the house *żurek* – a sour rye soup flavoured with sausage – served here in a bread bowl. (☎12 422 7601; www.kuchniaubabcimaliny. pl; ul Sławkowska 17; mains 12-25zł; ⏰11am-9pm Mon-Fri, noon-9pm Sat & Sun; 🚋2, 4, 14, 19, 20, 24)

U Babci Maliny – Szpitalna   POLISH €

26 🍴 Map p46, E3

The Szpitalna branch of arguably Kraków's most famous milk bar, 'Granny Raspberry's' is a godsend for travellers on a budget. Hearty Polish staples like soup, *pierogi* and potato pancakes are sold for giveaway prices and served in an overwrought boudoir-like basement eatery. (☎12 421 4818; www.kuchniaubabcimaliny.pl; ul Szpitalna 38; mains 10-25zł; ⏰noon-11pm)

Moo Moo Steak & Burger Club   STEAK €€€

27 🍴 Map p46, E5

Steakhouses are the rage in Kraków and this is one of the best. Standard cuts include tenderloin, porterhouse, top loin and ribeye. Non-steak mains include a duck breast, served with red lentils. There's a cheaper burger menu (20-30zł), with creative takes on old standards, like a veal burger served with marinated peppers. The modern interior is spare but casual. (📞531 007 097; www.moomoo.com.pl; ul Św Krzyża 15; mains 50-75zł; ⏰11am-11pm; 📶; 🚌3, 10, 19, 24, 52)

77 Sushi SUSHI €€

28 🍴 Map p46, A5

This small sushi bar is always hopping and is particularly popular with students from the nearby university. It offers a full range of sushi options, plus lots of choices for roll combinations as well as grilled rolls (called 'hot sets' here), including a mouth-watering grilled butterfish roll. (📞12 421 1094; www.77sushi.com; ul Św Anny 5; mains 30-50zł; ⏰noon-11pm; 🚌2, 13, 18, 20)

Indus Tandoori INDIAN €€

29 🍴 Map p46, C3

Reputed to be the best Indian restaurant in town, the Indus serves curries, tandoori dishes and classics such as chicken tikka in a long narrow dining room with gilded decor. (📞12 423 2282; www.indus.pl; ul Sławkowska 13/15; mains 20-35zł; ⏰noon-10pm Sun-Thu, noon-midnight Fri & Sat; 🚌2, 4, 14, 19, 24)

Green Day VEGETARIAN €

30 🍴 Map p46, D5

Some of Kraków's best-value vegetarian and vegan fare is on offer at this branch of a veggie chain, with meat-free burgers, wraps and salads on the menu. (📞12 431 1027; www.greenday.pl; ul Mikołajska 14; mains 9-22zł; ⏰11am-10pm Mon-Sat, to 9pm Sun; 🍴; 🚌3, 10, 19, 24, 52)

Understand

Austrians and the Planty

When the Kingdom of Poland was partitioned at the end of the 18th century, Kraków was grabbed up by the Austrians. The city's new Germanic administrators wanted to revamp the old Polish capital, making it less medieval Slavic and more imperial Habsburg. Decrepit dwellings, smelly stalls and charmless churches were torn down; leafy lanes, brawny bridges and sanitising sewers were built up. A main target of the reclamation project was the city's medieval wall. After five centuries, the brick barricade could no longer protect residents from modern artillery and siege tactics. The walls, towers and grandiose gates were dismantled, and the outer moats and trenches were filled in. In its place came a new green wall, a state-of-the-art park known as the Planty. Since the 1820s, the Planty has been the place to be in summer for residents seeking cool cover, with the poplars overhead and lush lawns underfoot.

Drinking

Café Bunkier
CAFE

31 Map p46, A4

The 'Bunker' is a wonderful cafe with a positively enormous glassed-in terrace tacked onto the Bunkier Sztuki (Art Bunker), a cutting-edge gallery northwest of the Rynek. The garden space is heated in winter and seems to always have a buzz. Excellent coffee, unfiltered beers, and homemade lemonades, as well as light bites like burgers and salads. Enter from the Planty. (📞12 431 0585; http://en.bunkiercafe.pl; Plac Szczepański 3a; ⏱9am-late; 🛜; 🚊2, 4, 14, 18, 20, 24)

Café Camelot
CAFE

32 Map p46, C4

For coffee and cake, try this genteel haven hidden around an obscure street corner in the Old Town. Its cosy rooms are cluttered with lace-covered candlelit tables, and a quirky collection of wooden figurines featuring spiritual or folkloric scenes. Also a great choice for breakfasts and brunches. (📞12 421 0123; www.camelot.pl; ul Św Tomasza 17; ⏱9am-midnight; 🚊2, 4, 14, 19, 20, 24)

Café Philo
CAFE

33 Map p46, E5

Black brick walls are lined with well-loved books and records. Worn leather furniture is populated by intellectual types who look like they might be plotting a revolution. Chatty bar staff and clientele reassure you that they are not. (ul Św Tomasza 30; ⏱10am-11.30pm Sun-Wed, to 3am Thu-Sat; 🛜; 🚊3, 10, 19, 24, 52)

Nowa Prowincja
CAFE

34 Map p46, B6

You'll love this bi-level bohemian cafe, where Kraków's coolest cats come to drink strong coffee and think deep thoughts. The original Prowincja (next door) still has hole-in-the-wall appeal, but head to the more spacious new outlet to order substantial food or sit at an old-fashioned school desk on the pavement. (📞693 770 079; ul Bracka 3/5; ⏱8.30am-11pm Mon-Sat, 9.30am-11pm Sun; 🚊1, 6, 8, 13, 18)

Antycafe
BAR

35 Map p46, C3

This popular Old Town student bar serves a full range of drinks and stays open late. Good place to start off or finish up the night. (📞506 481 888; www.antycafe.pl; ul Sławkowska 12; ⏱noon-late; 🛜; 🚊2, 4, 14, 18, 20, 24)

Ambasada Śledzia
BAR

36 Map p46, C6

The 'Herring Embassy' sits neatly, if cheekily, on this street lined with consulates. It's pioneered an unlikely but successful concept – herring and vodka shots. Sit at the bar and order tasty snack-sized servings of *śledź* (herring) or *kiełbasa* (sausage) to go

JOHN WARBURTON-LEE PHOTOGRAPHY/ALAMY ©

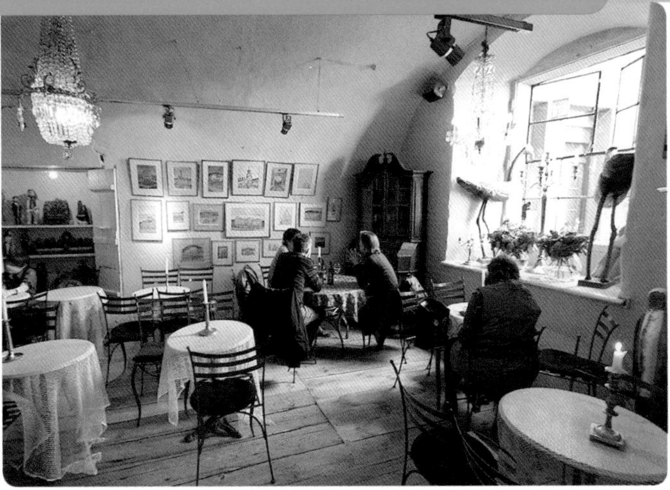

Café Camelot

with your vodka. A second branch across the street (ul Stolarska 5) stays open until 5am. (☎662 569 460; ul Stolarska 8-10; ⏰noon-midnight; 🚋1, 6, 8, 13, 18)

Tram Bar

BAR

37 Map p46, C6

Quirky bar in the middle of the Old Town's most popular drinking street. True to its name, Tram Bar is dedicated to the street car, with old maps and memorabilia on the walls and even seats made from old tram cars. Since it's not as overrun at night compared with neighbouring pubs, it's often possible to find a seat here. (☎12 423 2255; Stolarska 5; ⏰11am-2am; 🚋1, 6, 8, 13, 18)

Black Gallery

PUB

38 Map p46, E5

Underground pub-cum-nightclub with a modern aspect: split levels, exposed steel-frame lighting and a metallic bar. It really gets going after midnight. During the day, relax over beers in the courtyard. (☎724 630 154; ul Mikołajska 24; ⏰noon-late Mon-Sat, 2pm-late Sun; 📶; 🚋3, 10, 19, 24, 52)

Hush Live

CLUB

39 Map p46, C4

The latest incarnation at this legendary subterranean club space in the Old Town features DJs and bands that play a style of music called 'Disco

Polo' – essentially a Polish take on cheesy dance pop from the 1990s. Very popular and more fun than it sounds. (📞604 943 400; www.hushlive.pl; ul Św Tomasza 11; ⊗8pm-3am Sun-Thu, to 5am Fri & Sat; 🚊2, 4, 14, 19, 20, 24)

Frantic
CLUB

40 🚇 Map p46, B5

With two dance floors, three bars, a chill-out room and top Polish and international DJs, Frantic is regularly packed out with smart young locals. There's sniffy door selection, so don't be too scruffy. (📞12 423 0483; www.frantic. pl; ul Szewska 5; ⊗10pm-4am Wed-Sat; 🛜; 🚊2, 13, 18, 20)

PAWEL KAZMIERCZAK/SHUTTERSTOCK ©

Teatr im Słowackiego

Entertainment

Harris Piano Jazz Bar
JAZZ

41 ⭐ Map p46, B5

This active jazz haunt is housed in an atmospheric cellar space. Harris hosts jazz and blues bands most nights of the week from around 9.30pm, but try to arrive an hour earlier to get a seat (or book in advance by phone). Wednesday nights see (free) weekly jam sessions. (📞12 421 5741; www.harris.krakow.pl; Rynek Główny 28; ⊗1pm-late; 🚊1, 6, 8, 13, 18)

Stalowe Magnolie
LIVE MUSIC

42 ⭐ Map p46, D3

'Steel Magnolias' is a brightly decorated venue with an emphasis on live music, presenting pop, rock and jazz. It's a party inside every night of the week, with the music starting up around 9pm. Thursday night is ladies' night. (📞12 422 8472; www.stalowemagnolie.pl; ul Św Jana 15; ⊗7pm-late; 🛜; 🚊2, 4, 14, 18, 19, 24)

Teatr im Słowackiego
OPERA, THEATRE

43 ⭐ Map p46, E3

This important theatre focuses on Polish classics and large-scale productions. It's in a large and opulent building (1893) that's patterned on the Paris Opera, and is northeast of the Rynek Główny. (📞information 12 424 4528, tickets 12 424 4526; www.slowacki.krakow.pl; Plac Św Ducha 1; tickets 20-80zł; ⊗box office 10am-2pm & 2.30-6pm Mon, 9am-2pm & 2.30-7pm Tue-Sat, 3-7pm Sun; 🚊2, 3, 4, 10, 14, 19, 24, 52)

Re
LIVE MUSIC

44 Map p46, D6

You can't beat Re for its excellent line-up of live music, which features indie rock bands from all over the world, playing up close and in your face. Even if you're not into the music, you'll love the shady courtyard. (☑12 431 0881; www.klubre.pl; ul Św Krzyża 4; ☺noon-2am; ☒3, 10, 19, 24, 52)

Narodowy Stary Teatr
THEATRE

45 Map p46, B4

This is the city's best-known theatre company and it has attracted the cream of its actors. To overcome the language barrier, pick a Shakespeare play you know well from the repertoire, and take in the distinctive Polish interpretation. The box office is off Plac Szczepański. (☑12 422 8020; www.stary.pl; ul Jagiellońska 5; tickets adult/concession 55/35zł; ☺ box office 10am-1pm, 5-7pm Tue-Sat; ☒2, 4, 14, 18, 20, 24)

Bonerowski Palace
CONCERT VENUE

46 Map p46, C5

The Renaissance Hall of the Bonerowski Palace is home to regular evening piano recitals of music by Fryderyk Chopin, Poland's best-known composer. Check the website for details. Buy tickets at the venue or by telephone. (☑604 093 570; www.cracowconcerts.com; ul Św Jana 1; tickets 60zł; ☺7pm Tue-Sun; ☒1, 6, 8, 13, 18)

Jazz Club U Muniaka
JAZZ

47 Map p46, C5

Housed in a fine cellar, this is one of the best-known jazz outlets in Poland, the brainchild of saxophonist Janusz Muniak. There are concerts most nights from 8.30pm. (☑12 423 1205; www.umuniaka.pl; ul Floriańska 3; ☺7pm-late; 🛜; ☒2, 4, 14, 19, 20, 24)

Piec' Art
JAZZ

48 Map p46, A4

Dark and inviting, this intimate basement bar is a seductive place for a drink even when it's quiet. Several times a week, there's live acoustic jazz, which makes it all the more appealing. (☑12 429 1602; www.piecart.pl; ul Szewska 12; performances 15-20zł; ☺noon-late; 🛜; ☒2, 13, 18, 20)

Shopping

Galeria Dyląg
GALLERY

49 Map p46, E5

This small private art gallery features modern Polish artists from the 1940s to the 1970s. Look for the Polish drip paintings, reminiscent of Jackson Pollock, from the late '50s. Many of the pieces on sale here are from artists now displayed in museums. (☑12 431 2521; www.dylag.pl; ul Św Tomasza 22; ☺noon-6pm Mon-Fri, 11am-2pm Sat; ☒3, 10, 19, 24, 52)

Galeria Plakatu

LONELY PLANET/GETTY IMAGES ©

Galeria Plakatu ART

50 Map p46, C6

Poland has always excelled in the underrated art of making film posters and this amazing shop has the city's largest and best choice of posters, created by Poland's most prominent graphic artists. (☎12 421 2640; www.cracowposter-gallery.com; ul Stolarska 8-10; ☉11am-6pm Mon-Fri, to 2pm Sat; 🚋1, 6, 8, 13, 18)

Antykwariat Stefan Kamiński BOOKS

51 Map p46, C4

Evocative, dusty antiquarian bookshop with plenty of old post-

cards, prints, books and posters to rummage through. (☎12 422 3965; www.krakow-antykwariat.pl; ul Św Jana 3; ☉9am-5pm Mon-Fri, 10am-1.30pm Sat; 🚋1, 6, 8, 13, 18)

Wedel Pijalnia Czekolady FOOD & DRINK

52 Map p46, C5

The name E Wedel means only one thing: chocolate. This 'chocolate lounge' is the place to buy a box of handmade pralines to take home to your sweetheart. (☎12 429 4085; www.wedelpijalnie.pl; Rynek Główny 46; ☉9am-10pm; 🚋1, 6, 8, 13, 18)

Krakowski Kredens
FOOD & DRINK

53 🔒 Map p46, C6

If you love *żurek* like we love *żurek,* you'll want to take some home. Peek inside the 'Kraków cupboard' and you'll find a jar of this traditional sour rye soup, as well as loads of edible souvenirs, such as marinated mushrooms, herb honey, spicy mustard and gooseberry preserves. (☎12 423 8159; www.krakowskikredens.pl; ul Grodzka 7; ☉10am-8pm Mon-Sat, 11am-6pm Sun; 🚊1, 6, 8, 13, 18)

La Mama
CLOTHING

54 🔒 Map p46, C3

Local designer Monika shows off her funky children's fashions. Everything is made from natural fabrics and the designs are simple and clean. (☎602 396 230; www.lamama.sklep.pl; ul Sławkówska 24; ☉10am-7pm Mon-Fri, 11am-4pm Sat; 🚊2, 4, 14, 19, 20, 24)

My Gallery
JEWELLERY

55 🔒 Map p46, B6

This one little room has such an eclectic assortment you could do all your souvenir shopping here. Choose from dramatic, nature-inspired jewellery, handmade scarves and sweaters, and stained-glass sun catchers, as well as the odd pair of soft slippers. (☎12 431 1344; www.mygallery.pl; ul Gołębia 1a; ☉9am-7pm Mon-Fri, 10am-4pm Sat; 🚊2, 13, 18, 20)

Krakowska Manufaktura Czekolady
FOOD

56 🔒 Map p46, B5

Beautiful figurines made of white and dark chocolate, as well as a range of wrapped chocolate candies and caramels, including a life-sized chocolate Labrador (dog) that would take at least a month to eat. Upstairs there's a cafe for perfectly executed hot chocolate drinks as well as cakes, candies and coffee. (☎502 090 765; www.chocolate.krakow.pl; ul Szewska 7; ☉10am-10pm; 🚊2, 4, 14, 18, 24)

Jan Fejkiel Gallery
GALLERY

57 🔒 Map p46, C3

Jan Fejkiel was trained as an art historian, but his gallery specialises in contemporary prints and drawings, with a focus on emerging artists. This place claims the country's largest stock of contemporary graphic art, so he's not messing around. (☎12 429 1553; www.fejkielgallery.com; ul Sławkowska 14; ☉11am-6pm Mon-Fri, to 3pm Sat; 🚊2, 4, 14, 19, 20, 24)

Boruni Amber Museum
JEWELLERY

58 🔒 Map p46, C4

One-stop shopping for amberphiles. Cases and cases of amber rings, necklaces, brooches and earrings, plus a 'museum' (free admission) at the back, where you can see how amber is cut, polished and set. Boruni includes a certificate of quality with each purchase. (☎513 511 512; www.ambermuseum.eu; ul Św Jana 4; ☉10am-9pm; 🚊1, 6, 8, 13, 18)

Explore

Kazimierz

For much of its 700-year history, Kazimierz was an independent town with its own municipal charter and laws. Its mixed Jewish and Christian populations created a pair of distinctive communities side by side. These days, Kazimierz does double-duty. It's home to many important tourist attractions as well as some of the city's most-popular cafes, clubs and restaurants.

EUINKASOPOTNICKA/GETTY IMAGES ©

The Sights in a Day

☼ For the morning, focus your attention on the Jewish-themed sights in the eastern part of the neighbourhood. Grab a coffee at any cafe on **Plac Nowy** (p80). If you're hungry, **Le Scandale** (p77) has a very good breakfast buffet. Suitably sustained, find ul Józefa and wander along the tiny streets, taking in one or more of the **High** (p70), **Isaac** (p70) and **Remuh** (p70) synagogues, before visiting the **Galicia Jewish Museum** (p64).

☀ For a cheap and delicious lunch, there's the milk-bar side of **Sąsiedzi** (p74), or we love the hummus and grilled meats at **Hamsa** (p74). For the rest of the afternoon, shift your focus to the western – Catholic – side of Kazimierz taking in the **Corpus Christi Church** (p73) and impressive **St Catherine's** (p71). Spend the rest of the day **gallery hopping** (p66).

☾ Plan your evening meal at **Marchewka z Groszkiem** (p74) on trendy ul Mostowa and repair for drinks to **Miejsce Bar** (p78), **Singer** (p78) or **Mleczarnia** (p78). These places are all great and the evening could very well end up here, but if you've still got something left in the tank, check out the energetic dance floor at **Cocon Music Club** (p79).

For a local's day in Kazimierz, see p66.

👁 Top Sights
Galicia Jewish Museum (p64)

🔍 Local Life
Gallery Hopping in Kazimierz (p66)

💜 Best of Kraków
Food
Marchewka z Groszkiem (p74)

Momo (p75)

Sąsiedzi (p74)

Drinking & Nightlife
Cheder (p78)

Singer (p78)

Mleczarnia (p78)

Cocon Music Club (p79)

Jewish Heritage
High Synagogue (p70)

Isaac Synagogue (p70)

Jewish Museum (p70)

Remuh Cemetery (p71)

Getting There

🚋 **Trams** 3, 9, 19, 24 and 50 serve the eastern half of Kazimierz, close to the area of the former Jewish Ghetto.

🚋 **Trams** 6, 8, 10 and 13 run to the western part of the neighbourhood and stop near Plac Wolnica.

Top Sights
Galicia Jewish Museum

This excellent museum and research centre takes a different tack in exploring Jewish history and the impact of the Holocaust in the region. Instead of presenting objects from the past, the main exhibitions are built around contemporary photos, with corresponding text, of places and objects that once played an important role in Jewish culture and heritage. In many cases, these places no longer exist. The effect is to help us to see the past through the present day.

👁 Map p68, H2

📞 12 421 6842

www.galiciajewish
museum.org

ul Dajwór 18

adult/concession 15/10zł

🕙 10am-6pm

🚋 3, 9, 19, 24, 50

Don't Miss

'Traces of Memory'

The centrepiece of the museum is a moving photographic essay titled 'Traces of Memory: A Contemporary Look at the Jewish Past in Poland' that depicts modern-day remnants of the once-thriving Jewish community in the southeast of the country. The exhibition was the brainchild of the late photographer Chris Schwarz, together with academic Jonathan Webber.

'An Unfinished Memory'

The newest permanent exhibit, 'An Unfinished Memory: Jewish Heritage and the Holocaust in Eastern Galicia', employs the same photographic techniques used in Traces of Memory to explore Jewish history and memory – but pushes the geographic boundary to Eastern Galicia (today's Western Ukraine). Based on photos and text by Jason Francisco, the exhibit considers the con-tinuing impact of Jewish heritage in the region and how the Holocaust and its aftermath have af-fected the area's social and cultural development.

Temporary Exhibitions

The museum has carved out a reputation for staging important temporary exhibitions that complement the institution's purpose. Some of our favourite past shows include a series of video testimonies from Holocaust survivors and the exhi-bition 'Polish Heroes: Those Who Rescued Jews'.

Cultural Programme

The museum goes beyond the writ of standard his-tory museums by actively promoting and staging dramatic and musical performances. Many of these are timed to coincide with city festivals, such as the Festival of Jewish Culture, held in late June or early July. Consult the website for current events.

☑ Top Tips

▶ The museum also has one of the area's best bookshops, with plenty of titles on Polish and Galician history, Judaica and the Holocaust.

▶ Tours around Kazi-mierz and Podgórze as well as further afield to the Auschwitz-Birkenau Memorial & Museum are also available. Contact the museum by phone or email.

▶ This is one of the few important museums around town that are open on Mondays throughout the year. So you might want to save this one for Monday and visit other museums the rest of the week.

✗ Take a Break

Bagelmama (p77) has great bagel sandwiches and coffee for a quick pick-me-up. They also do light lunches, like wraps and bowls of chilli, in case you're looking for something a bit more substantial.

Local Life
Gallery Hopping in Kazimierz

Kazimierz is not only the go-to spot for nightlife and cafes; it's also great for hunting down quirky shops and galleries that go beyond the standard souvenir and amber shops. Rents are still low enough (though they're rising fast) to allow individual owners to hawk their own creations or to sell genuine antiques at junk-shop prices – though you'll need a good eye to distinguish the truly valuable from the merely interesting.

1 Dramatic Bowls and Vases

At **CAHA Art** (☎698 302 868; www.caha-art.pl; ul Brzozowa 17; ☺10.30am-6.30pm; ☒3, 9, 19, 24, 50), visual artist Katarzyna Gajda turns everyday items like plates, cups and bowls into dazzling bursts of colour and energy at this small ceramics gallery near the centre of Kazimierz. Each of the one-of-a-kind items is hand-sculpted and painted in pleasing mixes of fiery reds and mellower blues.

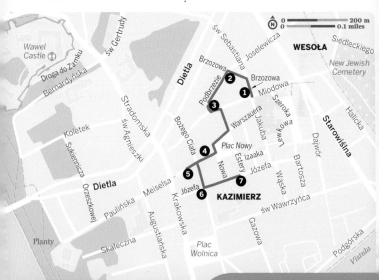

❷ Cubism to Socialist-Realism

Art curator Zofia Kruk has assembled a small but impressive collection of Polish paintings from the 1930s to the present day at her **Raven Gallery** (☏ 12 431 1129; www.raven.krakow.pl; ul Brzozowa 7; ☺ 11am-6pm Mon-Fri, to 3pm Sat; 🚋 11, 12, 22, 52). The gallery is particularly strong on Polish cubist paintings from the 1920s and '30s, as well as abstract and Socialist-Realist painting from the 1950s and '60s.

❸ Vintage Postcards

Galeria LueLue (☏ 728 551 024; www.luelue.pl; ul Miodowa 22; ☺ 10am-6m Mon-Fri, 10am-4pm Sat & Sun; 🚋 6, 8, 10, 13) specialises in vintage photographs, including stunning black and whites of life in Kraków in the 1920s and '30s. Most of what's on offer are affordable copies, but there are some originals as well. There's a huge selection of retro postcards and old posters.

❹ The Genuine Article

The **Danutta Hand Gallery** (☏ 733 466 277; www.danuttahandgallery.pl; ul Meiselsa 22; ☺ 10am-7pm Mon-Sat; 🚋 6, 8, 10, 13) appears to be an ordinary souvenir shop from the street, but it's actually a highly personalised boutique, featuring a range of original handicrafts made by local artists and artisans. We loved the cufflinks made from watch parts and earrings created from found objects.

❺ Retro Fashion

Vanilla (☏ 500 542 114; ul Meiselsa 7; ☺ 11am-7pm Mon-Fri, to 4pm Sat, 10am-3pm Sun; 🚋 6, 8, 10, 13) sells high-end, second-hand women's clothing from well-known international designers at a fraction of what the goods originally fetched in luxury boutiques. The owner has an excellent eye for vintage that still looks fresh. There's a nice range of tops, skirts, dresses, shoes and accessories.

❻ Contemporary Design

A self-described 'concept' store, whatever that means, **Marka** (☏ 12 422 2965; ul Józefa 5; ☺ noon-6pm; 🚋 6, 8, 10, 13) has a mission to promote the very best Polish design in poster art, lighting, glassware, ceramics, furniture and household items. Standouts include retro lighting fixtures, beautifully sculpted vases, and crystal decanters and bowls.

❼ High-End Jewellery

The eye-catching creations of Grzegorz Błażko are on display at **Błażko Jewellery Design** (☏ 508 646 298; www.blazko.pl; ul Józefa 11; ☺ 11am-7pm Mon-Fri, to 3pm Sat; 🚋 6, 8, 10, 13), a small gallery and workshop right in the heart of Kazimierz's gallery area on ul Józefa. Even if you're not buying, pop in to take a look at the designer's unique range of chequered enamel rings, pendants, bracelets, earrings, and cufflinks. Most are set in silver.

A Wawel Hill

B

C

D **KAZIMIERZ**

1

Bernardyńska

Stradomska

Smocza

Koletek

Koletek

św Agnieszki

Dietla

2

Statek Nimfa
⊙ 11

Sukiennicza

Meiselsa

Dietla

Orzeszkowej

Paulińska

St Catherine's Church
◉ 6

3

Most Grunwaldzki

św Stanisława

Kordeckiego

Augustiańska

Skałeczna

Vistula

Paulińska

Pauline Church of SS Michael & Stanislaus
7 ◉

Piekarska

4

DĘBNIKI

For reviews see

◉	Top Sights	p64
◉	Sights	p70
✕	Eating	p74
🍷	Drinking	p78
🔒	Shopping	p80

Skawińska

Wietora

5

Ⓝ 0 —————— 200 m
0 —————— 0.1 miles

E

Dietla

New Jewish Cemetery

Podbrzezie

Brzozowa

Miodowa

Starowiślna

WESOŁA

Halicka

F

G

H

1

21 39

18

Dajwór

Rzeszowska

13

Remuh Cemetery

5

Remuh Synagogue

4

33

28

Warszauera

Jakuba

Lewkowa

Szeroka

31

19

Bożego Ciała Miodowa

14

41

26

25

30

35

Plac Nowy

3 Isaac Synagogue

2

1 Jewish Museum

22

Galicia Jewish Museum

2

23

27

40

Estery

Izaaka

High Synagogue

Nowa

29

Józefa

16

Bartosza

Wąska

24

3

37

17

Krakowska

Józefa

Bożego Ciała

InfoKraków Kazimierz

św Wawrzyńca

10

Museum of Municipal Engineering

Corpus Christi Church

8

34

15

36

9 Ethnographic Museum

Plac Wolnica

Bocheńska

Mostowa

20

12

Bonifraterska

Gazowa

Podgórska

4

Trynitarska

Mostowa

38

32

Vistula

5

Podgórska

Kładka Bernatka

Sights

Jewish Museum

MUSEUM

1 ⦿ Map p68, G2

This museum is housed in the Old Synagogue, which dates to the 15th century. The prayer hall, complete with a reconstructed *bimah* (raised platform at the centre where the Torah is read) and the original *aron kodesh* (the niche in the eastern wall where Torah scrolls are kept), houses an exhibition of liturgical objects. Upstairs there's a photographic exhibit. (Old Synagogue; ☑12 422 0962; www.mhk.pl; ul Szeroka 24; adult/concession 9/7zł, free Mon; ⊘10am-2pm Mon, 9am-5pm Tue-Sun; ⊟3, 9, 19, 24, 50)

☑ Top Tip

Jewish Heritage Tours

To get more out of the Jewish heritage sites of Kazimierz it can help to have a guide. The **Jarden Tourist Agency** (Map p68, G1; ☑12 421 7166; www.jarden.pl; ul Szeroka 2; ⊟3, 9, 19, 24, 50) runs two- and three-hour walking tours of Kazimierz and Podgórze, as well as a popular two-hour driving tour of places made famous by the film *Schindler's List*. Tours are priced per person and range from 40zł to 90zł depending on the number of people participating. The Galicia Jewish Museum (p64) also offers guided tours of the area. Contact the museum for details.

High Synagogue

SYNAGOGUE

2 ⦿ Map p68, G2

This place of worship was built around 1560, and is the third-oldest synagogue in Kraków after the Old and Remuh Synagogues. The High Synagogue takes its name from the fact that the prayer hall was situated on the 1st floor, while the ground floor was given over to shops. These days, the ground floor holds arguably the city's best Jewish bookshop, Austeria (p81). (Synagoga Wysoka; ☑12 430 6889; www.austeria.eu; ul Józefa 38; adult/concession 9/6zł; ⊘9.30am-7pm; ⊟3, 9, 19, 24, 50)

Isaac Synagogue

SYNAGOGUE

3 ⦿ Map p68, G2

Near the southwestern edge of the Remuh Cemetery is Kraków's largest synagogue, completed in 1644. In the wake of WWII, it was finally returned to the Jewish community in 1989. Inside you can see the remains of the original stuccowork and wall-painting decoration. The synagogue was recently restored and now houses a permanent exhibition titled 'In Memory of Polish Jews'. (Synagoga Izaaka; ☑12 430 2222; ul Jakuba 25, enter from Kupa 18; adult/concession 10/7zł; ⊘9am-7pm Sun-Thu, to 2.30pm Fri; ⊟3, 9, 19, 24, 50)

Remuh Synagogue

SYNAGOGUE

4 ⦿ Map p68, G1

Near the northern end of ul Szeroka is the district's smallest synagogue and one of only two in the area that is

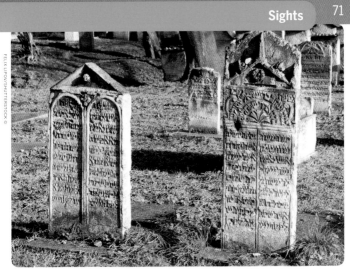

FELIX LIPOV/SHUTTERSTOCK ©

Remuh Cemetery

regularly used for religious services. The synagogue was established in 1558 by a rich merchant, Israel Isserles, and is also associated with his son Rabbi Moses Isserles, a philosopher and scholar. (📞12 430 5411; www.remuh.jewish. org.pl; ul Szeroka 40; adult/concession 5/2zł; ⏰9am-6pm Sun-Thu; 🚊3, 9, 19, 24, 50)

Remuh Cemetery   CEMETERY

5 ◎ Map p68, G1

Just behind the Remuh Synagogue and founded in the mid-16th century, this cemetery was closed for burials in the late 18th century, when a new, larger graveyard was established. During WWII the German occupiers vandalised and razed the tombstones,

but during postwar conservation work some 700 gravestones, many outstanding Renaissance examples that dated back four centuries, were uncovered. The tombstones have been meticulously restored, making the place one of the best-preserved Renaissance Jewish cemeteries anywhere in Europe. (📞12 430 5411; ul Szeroka 40; admission free; ⏰9am-6pm Mon-Thu; 🚊3, 9, 19, 24, 50)

St Catherine's Church   CHURCH

6 ◎ Map p68, D3

One of the most monumental churches in the city, and possibly the one that has best retained its original Gothic shape, St Catherine's was founded in 1363 and completed 35 years later,

Understand
The Story of Kazimierz

Kazimierz is mainly known these days as the former Jewish ghetto and the setting for the film *Schindler's List*, but it has an even richer history.

Once a Separate Town
The area's origins go back nearly seven centuries, when it was founded as a mainly-Christian town by King Kazimierz III Wielki on the southern fringe of Kraków. Thanks to numerous privileges granted by the king, the town developed swiftly and soon had its own town hall, two huge churches and a market square (today's Plac Wolnica) almost as large as Kraków's own.

By the end of the 14th century, Kazimierz was second only to Kraków in importance.

Jews and Christians Side By Side
The first Jews came to settle in Kazimierz soon after its founding, but it wasn't until 1494, when they were expelled from within the walls of Kraków by King Jan I Olbracht, that their numbers began to grow significantly. They settled in a prescribed area of Kazimierz, northeast of the Christian quarter, and the two sectors were separated by a wall.

The subsequent history of Kazimierz was punctuated by fires, floods and plagues. Although the Christian and Jewish communities lived side by side, the Jewish quarter grew particularly quickly. Kazimierz became a destination for Jews fleeing persecution from all corners of Europe, and this population gradually determined the character of the whole town. It became the most important Jewish centre in all of Poland.

The Darkest Days
At the outbreak of WWII, Kazimierz was a predominantly Jewish suburb, with a distinct culture and atmosphere. The Nazi occupation during the war would drastically alter the neighbourhood, as most of the city's 65,000 Jews were killed during the Holocaust.

During communist rule, Kazimierz was largely a forgotten district of Kraków, and descended into something of a slum. Then, in the early 1990s, along came Steven Spielberg to shoot *Schindler's List* and everything changed overnight. By day or by night, it's now one of the city's most interesting and liveliest areas.

though its planned towers were never built. The lofty and spacious white-washed interior boasts the imposing, richly gilded Baroque high altar from 1634 and some flamboyant choir stalls. (Kościół św. Katarzyny; www.parafia-kazimierz.augustianie.pl; ul Augustiańska 7; ⏱10am-4pm Mon-Fri, 11am-2pm Sat; 🚊6, 8, 10, 13)

Pauline Church of SS Michael & Stanislaus   CHURCH

7 ◎ Map p68, B4

This mid-18th-century Baroque church is associated with Bishop Stanisław (Stanislaus) Szczepanowski, patron saint of Poland. In 1079, the bishop was beheaded by King Bolesław Śmiały (Boleslaus the Bold): the tree trunk where the deed was done is next to the altar. The crypt shelters the tombs of 12 eminent cultural figures, including the Nobel-winning writer and poet Czesław Miłosz. (Skałka Kościół Paulinów Św Michała i Stanisława; ☎12 619 0900; www.skalka.paulini.pl; ul Skałeczna 15; adult/concession 3/2zł; ⏱9am-5pm; 🚊6, 8, 10, 13)

Corpus Christi Church   CHURCH

8 ◎ Map p68, F3

In the northeastern corner of Plac Wolnica and founded in 1340, this was the first church in Kazimierz and for a long time the town's parish church. Its interior has been almost totally fitted out with Baroque furnishings, including the huge high altar, extraordinary massive carved stalls in the chancel and a boat-shaped pulpit. Note the surviving early-15th-century

stained-glass window in the sanctuary and the crucifix hanging above the chancel. (Parafia Bożego Ciała w Krakowie; ☎12 430 5995; www.bozecialo.net; ul Bożego Ciała 26; ⏱7am-7pm; 🚊6, 8, 10, 13)

Ethnographic Museum   MUSEUM

9 ◎ Map p68, E4

This interesting museum is housed within the former town hall of Kazimierz. It was built in the late 14th century then significantly extended in the 16th century, at which time it acquired its Renaissance appearance. The permanent exhibition features the reconstructed interiors of traditional Polish peasant cottages and workshops, folk costumes, craft and trade exhibits, extraordinary nativity scenes, and folk and religious painting and woodcarving. (Muzeum Etnograficzne; ☎12 430 5575; www.etnomuzeum.eu; Plac Wolnica 1; adult/concession 13/7zł; free Sun; ⏱11am-7pm Tue, Wed, Fri & Sat, to 9pm Thu, to 3pm Sun; 🚊6, 8, 10, 13)

Museum of Municipal Engineering   MUSEUM

10 ◎ Map p68, G3

Tramcars and trucks fill the courtyard of this former depot, while inside there's a small collection of cars and motorbikes. A room of hands-on magnetic and water experiments is sure to keep kids occupied, too. (Muzeum Inżynierii Miejskiej; ☎12 421 1242; www.mimk.com.pl; Św Wawrzyńca 15; adult/child 10/7zł; ⏱10am-4pm Tue-Sun; 🚊3, 9, 19, 24, 50)

Statek Nimfa

CRUISE

11 ⊙ Map p68, A2

The pleasure boat *Nimfa* cruises along the Vistula River, departing from the pier below Wawel Castle, and motoring past sights such as Kościuszko Mound, Skałka and Plac Bohaterów Getta, with up-close views of all six bridges. The three-hour tour goes all the way to Tyniec. Book tickets online or by email. (☑505 102 677; www.statekkrakow.com; Wawel pier; 1hr cruise adult/concession 25/20zł, 3hr cruise 60/50zł; ☺10am-6pm; 🚊11, 18, 22, 52)

⬤ Local Life
'Polish Pizza'

Kazimierz is the spiritual home of one of Poland's most beloved snack foods: *zapiekanka* (sometimes referred to jokingly as 'Polish pizza'). The idea is simple. It's a half of a baguette, topped with cheese, ham and mushrooms. Other varieties are available (the 'Hawaiian' has ham and pineapple), but nothing beats the classic. It's a cheap, filling snack that tastes especially delicious after midnight. Indeed, there may be no reason to eat it before midnight. The place to find it is the round brick building – the *Okrąglak* – at the centre of **Plac Nowy** (Map p68, F2). The rotunda was built in 1900 as a marketplace. These days, it serves the important function of a late-night food court that stays open into the wee hours to cater to carousers from the local clubs and pubs.

Eating

Marchewka z Groszkiem

POLISH €€

12 ⊗ Map p68, F4

Traditional Polish cooking, with hints of influence from neighbouring countries like Ukraine (beer), Hungary (wine) and Lithuania. Excellent potato pancakes and a delicious boiled beef with horseradish sauce highlight the menu. There's are a few sidewalk tables to admire the parade of people down one of Kazimierz's up-and-coming streets. (☑12 430 0795; www.marchewkazgroszkiem.pl; ul Mostowa 2; mains 20-30zł; ☺9am-10pm; 🛜; 🚊6, 8, 10, 13)

Sąsiedzi

POLISH €€€

13 ⊗ Map p68, F1

A perfect combination: on the left side a high-end Polish restaurant with a secluded garden, while on the right a clean, friendly milk bar, serving well-above-average steam table food at affordable prices. We love the roast duck in apple with pearl barley (47zł) at the restaurant. Evening meals are accompanied by live piano music. Reservations (for the fancier side) are recommended. (☑12 654 8353; www.sasiedzi.oberza.pl; ul Miodowa 25; mains 30-50zł, milk bar 10-20zł; ☺10am-10pm; 🛜; 🚊3, 9, 19, 24, 50)

Hamsa

JEWISH €€

Located next to the Jarden Jewish Bookshop (see 39 🔖 Map p68, G1), Hamsa has a light, uncluttered interior and

LONELY PLANET/GETTY IMAGES ©

Klezmer-Hois (p76)

is a welcome tonic to the, admittedly kitschy, Jewish-themed restaurants in the area. The menu features a full range of Middle Eastern salads, plus spicy grilled chicken and fish, as well as a good selection of vegetarian and gluten-free options. How can a place miss when it calls itself a 'hummus and happiness' restaurant? (📞515 150 145; www.hamsa.pl; ul Szeroka 2; mains 30-50zł; ⏰10am-11pm; 📶🍴; 🚊3, 9, 19, 24, 50)

Momo   VEGETARIAN €

14 🍴 Map p68, E2

Vegans will cross the doorstep of this restaurant with relief – the majority of the menu is animal-free. The space is decorated with Indian craft pieces, and serves up subcontinental soups, stuffed

pancakes and rice dishes, with a great range of cakes – some gluten-free. The *momo* (Tibetan dumplings; 15zł) are a treat worth ordering. (📞609 685 775; ul Dietla 49; mains 12-19zł; ⏰11am-8pm; 🍴; 🚊11, 12, 22, 52)

Młynek Café   VEGETARIAN €

15 🍴 Map p68, F4

This vegetarian cafe is the perfect pit stop on the 'other' side of Kazimierz. It offers delectable, animal-free soups and sandwiches; occasional concerts, poetry readings and art exhibits; a collection of typewriters and coffee grinders to admire; and outdoor seating overlooking the square. (📞12 430 6202; www. cafemlynek.com; Plac Wolnica 7; mains 15-20zł; ⏰8am-11pm; 📶🍴; 🚊6, 8, 10, 13)

Kuchnia i Wino
MEDITERRANEAN €€

16 Map p68, F3

The name, 'Cuisine and Wine', may not suggest this bistro has a lot of imagination, however the delightfully inspired Mediterranean menu is unusual in Kraków, featuring handmade pasta and fresh seafood. It's hard to resist the lovely garden setting, while the interior, with its sky-painted ceiling and Tuscan tones, is also inviting. (☑12 430 6710; www.kuchniaiwino.eu; ul Józefa 13; mains 30-50zł; ☺noon-11pm; ☎; 🚋3, 9, 19, 24, 50)

Deli Bar
HUNGARIAN €€

17 Map p68, E3

This unassuming bar hides what in fact is a very good Hungarian restaurant. The Hungarian owners turn out tasty paprika-laced classics such as goulash, *palacsinta* (crepes) and 'Budapest pork'. (☑12 430 6404; ul Meiselsa 5; mains 15-40zł; ☺1pm-10pm; 🚋6, 8, 10, 13)

Klezmer-Hois
JEWISH €€

18 Map p68, G1

More than any other restaurant, Klezmer-Hois evokes pre-war Kazimierz, with its tables covered in lace, and artwork inspired by the shtetl (Jewish town). Warm up with a bowl of delicious soup invented by Yankiel the Innkeeper of Berdytchov. In the evenings, folks gather for concerts of traditional Jewish music (8pm). (☑12 411 1245; www.klezmer.pl; ul Szeroka 6; mains 30-40zł; ☺10am-9.30pm; 🚋3, 9, 19, 24, 50)

Ariel
JEWISH €€

19 Map p68, G2

One of a number of Jewish restaurants in and around ul Szeroka, this atmospheric joint is packed with old-fashioned timber furniture and portraits, and serves a range of kosher dishes. Try the Berdytchov soup (beef, honey and cinnamon) for a tasty starter. There's often live klezmer music here at night. (☑12 421 7920; www.ariel-krakow.pl; ul Szeroka 18; mains 20-60zł; ☺10am-midnight; ☎; 🚋3, 9, 19, 24, 50)

Well Done
BARBECUE €€

20 Map p68, F4

Very likable barbecue and burger joint poised along shady ul Mostowa, a string of restaurants and cafes that locals regard as the centre of Kazimierz's emerging hipsterdom. The grill masters know how to impart that smoky flavour to burgers, steaks and chicken breasts. The interior is kind of retro-diner, while there are a few picnic tables out front. (☑607 132 001; ul Mostowa 2; mains 15-30zł; ☺10am-11pm; ☎; 🚋6, 8, 10, 13)

Dawno Temu Na Kazimierzu
JEWISH €€

21 Map p68, G1

Arguably the smallest and most atmospheric of several restaurants in Kazimierz playing on the old-time Jewish theme. The traditional Polish-Jewish cooking (think hearty variations of lamb and duck) is very good, and the warm, candlelit space, with klezmer music playing in the background, make this the perfect spot to enjoy this part of Kraków. (Once upon a Time in Kazimierz; ☎12 421 2117; www.dawnotemu.nakazimierzu.pl; ul Szeroka 1; mains 20-35zł; ⏰10am-midnight; 🚋3, 9, 19, 24, 50)

Bagelmama

BAGELS €

22 Map p68, H2

How clever of someone to think of selling bagels in the Jewish quarter. Whether you are a bagel traditionalist (lox and cream cheese) or a bagel innovator (warm brie and tomato), you'll find something you like. There are also soups, salads, and wraps for a perfect easy lunch. (☎12 346 1646; www.bagelmama.com; Dajwór 10; sandwiches 15zł; ⏰9am-7pm; 📶; 🚋3, 9, 19, 24, 50)

Pierogi Mr Vincent

POLISH €

23 Map p68, E2

There are only a few scattered tables in this place, but there are about 40 kinds of dumplings on the menu; sweet and savoury, classic and creative. Maybe you thought you were tired of *pierogi* (dumplings), but Vincent will convince you to eat one more plate! (☎506 806 304; Bożego Ciała 12; mains 10-15zł; ⏰11am-9pm; 🚋6, 8, 10, 13)

Corner Burger

BURGERS €

24 Map p68, H3

Casual Brooklyn-inspired burger bar, featuring a range of freshly made burgers. Order at the counter and grab one of the handful of tables or booths. The setting, with exposed-white-brick walls and *Pulp Fiction* posters here and there, was designed for a quick bite or easy lunch on the run. The Polish Pride burger (18zł) includes a piece of sausage on top. (☎535 850 109; www.cornerburger.pl; ul Dajwór 25; burgers 15zł-20zł; ⏰11am-10pm Mon-Wed, to 11pm Thu-Sun; 🚋3, 9, 19, 24, 50)

Le Scandale

INTERNATIONAL €€

25 Map p68, F2

Part restaurant, part late-night lounge, complete with tucked-away booths, low-slung leather couches and a gleaming, well-stocked bar. Two elements are worth recommending: an all-you-can-eat breakfast bar (22zł) from 8am-noon and a hidden garden at the back, perfect for al fresco dining in warm weather. The menu runs the gamut from burgers and pasta to steaks and tapas. (☎12 430 6855; http://lescandale.pl; Plac Nowy 9; mains 25-32zł; ⏰8am-3am; 📶; 🚋6, 8, 10, 13)

Local Life

Food Trucks

A **hidden courtyard** (Map p68, G3; ul Św Wawrzyńca 16, Skwer Judah; most items 5-15zł; ⏰noon-10pm Tue-Thu, to 1am Fri-Sun; 🚋3, 9, 19, 24, 50) in Kazimierz just happens to be ground-zero for the city's emerging food-truck scene. Most days you'll catch trucks selling burgers, ice cream, sausages, stuffed potatoes and the current crowd favourite, Belgian fries (9zł). Especially popular at night, so go early or expect to queue up.

Drinking

Alchemia
CAFE

26 🚊 Map p68, F2

This Kazimierz venue exudes a shabby-is-the-new-cool look with rough-hewn wooden benches, candlelit tables and a companionable gloom. It hosts occasional live-music gigs and theatrical events through the week. (☎12 421 2200; www.alchemia. com.pl; ul Estery 5; ⊙9am-late; 🚊3, 9, 19, 24, 50)

Cheder
CAFE

Located at the High Synagogue (see 2 ◉ Map p68, G2), Cheder, unlike most of the other Jewish-themed places in Kazimierz, aims to entertain *and* educate. Named after a traditional Hebrew school, the cafe offers access to a decent library in Polish and English, regular readings and films, as well as real Israeli coffee, brewed in a traditional Turkish copper pot with cinnamon and cardamom, and snacks like homemade hummus. (☎515 732 226; www.cheder.pl; ul Józefa 36; ⊙10am-10pm; 🚊3, 9, 19, 24, 50)

Mleczarnia
CAFE

27 🚊 Map p68, E2

Wins the prize for best courtyard cafe – located across the street. Shady trees and blooming roses make this place tops for a sunny-day drink. If it's rainy, never fear, for the cafe is warm and cosy, with crowded bookshelves and portrait-covered walls. Self service. (☎12 421 8532; www.mle.pl; ul Meiselsa 20; ⊙10am-midnight; 🚊6, 8, 10, 13)

Miejsce Bar
BAR

28 🚊 Map p68, F1

Trendy bar that draws an eclectic mix of intellectual types, hipsters, students and generally anyone who enjoys good cocktails and a relaxed vibe. Quiet during the day; rowdier and more adventurous by night. (☎600 960 876; www.miejsce.com.pl; ul Estery 1; ⊙10am-2am; 🛜; 🚊11, 12, 22, 52)

Singer Café
BAR

29 🚊 Map p68, F2

A laid-back hang-out of the Kazimierz cognoscenti, this relaxed cafe-bar's moody candlelit interior is full of character. Alternatively, sit outside and converse over a sewing machine affixed to the table. (☎12 292 0622; ul Estery 20; ⊙9am-late; 🛜; 🚊3, 9, 19, 24, 50)

Bar Atelier
CAFE

30 🚊 Map p68, E2

Tucked into the corner of Plac Nowy, it's easy to miss this place, but don't pass it by. Krakovians rave about this luscious, laid-back little bar. It's hip enough to impress a date, but friendly enough that you want to return again and again. Decent light food, like burgers, and a sweet, hidden garden at the back. (☎690 866 800; Plac Nowy 71/2; ⊙3pm-2am; 🛜; 🚊6, 8, 10, 13)

Propaganda bar

Artefakt Cafe
CAFE

31 Map p68, H2

This much-loved student cafe has two front rooms and a small garden at the back. Bookshelves line the walls of one room, while big photos – part of a rotating photo exhibition – hang in the other. In addition to coffee drinks, they have a large selection of bottled craft beers and decent Czech lagers like Holba on tap. (535 799 666; www.artefakt-cafe.pl; ul Dajwór 3; 4pm-2am; 3, 9, 19, 24, 50)

Cocon Music Club
GAY & LESBIAN

32 Map p68, G5

One of the very few big gay clubs in Kraków, this Kazimierz bar and dance club has two rooms, one with electronic music, the other more popular disco. Thursdays are given over to karaoke, while Fridays see a popular 'old disco' party. (12 632 2296; www.klub-cocon.pl; ul Gazowa 21; 8pm-late; ; 6, 8, 10, 13)

Propaganda
BAR

33 Map p68, E1

This is another one of those places full of communist nostalgia, but so real are the banners and mementos here that we almost started singing the 'Internationale'. Also has a range of killer cocktails. (600 331 922; www.pubpropaganda.pl; ul Miodowa 20; noon-late; 3, 9, 19, 24, 50)

LaF
GAY & LESBIAN

34 Map p68, F4

This Kazimierz disco is one of the few lesbian clubs in Kraków, though the oldies and disco nights draw a mixed crowd and everyone seems to have a great time. Enter through the main door of the Młynek Café and descend a set of stairs. (607 307 121; Plac Wolnica 7; 10pm-5am Fri & Sat; 6, 8, 10, 13)

Shopping

Plac Nowy Flea Market
MARKET

35 Map p68, F2

Sometimes called the Jewish Market, this flea market is best on Saturday and Sunday mornings, when it's crammed with stalls selling everything from clothing to comic books. On other days, you'll find scattered tables with fresh produce, antiques,

---

✔ Top Tip

Jewish Culture Festival

The annual **Festival of Jewish Culture** (www.jewishfestival.pl), held in late June and early July, is the high point of Kazimierz's cultural calendar. Spread out over 10 days, the event brings in musical performances, film screenings, poetry readings, discussions and happenings of all sorts. The festival ends the final Saturday night with a big bash on ul Szeroka featuring traditional Jewish folk music.

---

and Judaism- and communism-related souvenirs. Late-night food stalls here operate until around 2am. (Jewish Market; Plac Nowy; from 6am; 6, 8, 10, 13)

Produkty Benedyktyńskie
FOOD & DRINK

36 Map p68, E4

The Benedictine monks are nothing if not industrious. Here you can buy cheeses, wines, cookies, honey...all the goodies that are produced by the holy men up the river in Tyniec, as well as some products from monasteries further afield. (Benedictine Products; 12 422 0216; www.produktybenedyktynskie.com; ul Krakowska 29; 9am-6pm Mon-Fri, to 3pm Sat; 6, 8, 10, 13)

By Insomnia
CLOTHING

37 Map p68, E3

Natural materials and subtly sexy styles characterise the designs for women's clothing on display at this tiny boutique. The flagship designer is Warsaw-based 'By Insomnia', and all of the clothing is made in Poland. (881 228 122; www.byinsomnia.com; ul Meiselsa 7; 10am-6pm Mon-Fri, to 3pm Sat; 6, 8, 10, 13)

Klubczyk
FOOD & DRINK

38 Map p68, G5

This tiny deli and packaged food shop on Kazimierz's blossoming ul Mostowa specialises in organic foods, including meats, cheeses, grains and beans of Polish origin. It's a handy shop for picking up picnic provisions. There's also a tiny retro-style cafe, with a few tables where you can sample the products in-house. (☎692 428 510; Mostowa 14; ◷10am-5pm Mon-Fri, 11am-6pm Sat & Sun; ◳6, 8, 10, 13)

Jarden Jewish Bookshop BOOKS

39 🔒 Map p68, G1

This small bookshop is dedicated to titles on Jewish heritage, with a decent selection on local history and lore, as well as Holocaust literature. It also sells Jewish-themed music on CDs, and offers tours of sites of Jewish interest. (☎12 421 7166; www.jarden.pl; ul Szeroka 2; ◷9am-6pm Mon-Fri, 10am-6pm Sat & Sun; ◳3, 9, 19, 24, 50)

Austeria BOOKS

Located at the High Synagogue (see 2 ◉ Map p68, G2), Austeria has the best collection of Jewish-themed books and Judaica in Kraków. (www.austeria.pl; ul Józefa 38; ◷9am-7pm; ◳3, 9, 19, 24, 50)

Antykwariat na Kazimierzu ANTIQUES

40 🔒 Map p68, F2

In the basement of the Judaica Foundation in Kazimierz, this Aladdin's cave is a jumble of antique china, glass, paintings, books and other assorted goodies. (☎12 292 6153; www.judaica.pl; ul Meiselsa 17; ◷10am-5pm Mon-Fri, to 2pm Sat & Sun; ◳6, 8, 10, 13)

Antyki Galeria Retro ANTIQUES

41 🔒 Map p68, E2

Bustling junk shop, featuring stacks of antique porcelain plates, silver sets, and candelabras on the tables, plus rows of big wooden clocks on the walls. There's also a small but well-curated selection of paintings from the 1960s and '70s. (☎691 803 863; www.antykiretro.pl; ul Miodowa 4; ◷11am-6pm Mon-Fri, 10.30am-3pm Sat; ◳6, 8, 10, 13)

Explore

Podgórze

This largely working-class suburb would receive few visitors if it wasn't for the notorious role it played during WWII. It was here the Nazis herded 16,000 Jews into a ghetto before sending them off to concentration camps. A smattering of sites recall these events, including the factory of Oskar Schindler, where many lives were saved. These days, the district is on the upswing as clubs and cafes start opening up.

AGNES KANTARUK/SHUTTERSTOCK ©

The Sights in a Day

☀ Grab a coffee at **BAL** (p91) or **Kącik 6** (p92), near **Schindler's Factory** (p84), and set aside the morning for sites related to Podgórze's dark days. In addition to the museum in the factory, check out the **Museum of Contemporary Art** (pictured left; p89) next door. Return to **Plac Bohaterów Getta** for one more must-see, the moving museum at the **Pharmacy Under the Eagle** (p89).

☀ In the afternoon, set aside a few hours to explore Podgórze's more mysterious side. Hike up the hill to see the ancient **Church of St Benedict** (p87), whose origins remain unknown. Check out the old Austrian stronghold, **St Benedict Fort** (p87), and then cross the highway to find the truly mysterious **Krakus Mound** (p87). Peer into the abandoned **Liban Quarry** (p87), where much of *Schindler's List* was actually filmed, to see elements of the old set that are still standing.

☾ For the evening, book a table at **ZaKładka Food & Wine** (p90) for some of the best Parisian bistro-style food the city has to offer. For live music, on weekend evenings try **Fabryka** (p93), while the dance nights at **Drukarnia** (p92) on Fridays and Saturday tend to run late.

For a local's day in Podgórze, see p86.

◉ Top Sights
Schindler's Factory (p84)

◯ Local Life
Podgórze's Quirkier Side (p86)

🖤 Best of Kraków

Food
ZaKładka Food & Wine (p90)

Music
Fabryka Klub (p93)

Art
Museum of Contemporary Art in Kraków (p89)

Architecture
Forum Przestrzenie (p92)

Shopping
Starmach Gallery (p93)

Jewish Heritage
Schindler's Factory (p84)

Getting There

🚋 **Trams** 3, 9, 19, 24 and 50 serve Plac Bohaterów Getta, the main jumping off spot for Schindler's Factory.

🚋 **Trams** 6, 8, 10 and 13 connect Podgórze to the western end of Kazimierz.

Top Sights
Schindler's Factory

An impressive interactive museum that goes well beyond its name and covers all aspects of the Nazi occupation of Kraków during WWII. It's housed in the former enamel factory of Oskar Schindler, the Nazi industrialist who saved the lives of more than 1000 members of his Jewish labour force during the Holocaust – a story made famous in Steven Spielberg's 1993 film *Schindler's List*.

👁 Map p88, E2

📞 12 257 0096

www.mhk.pl

ul Lipowa 4

adult/concession 21/16zł, free Mon

🕙 10am-4pm Mon, 9am-8pm Tue-Sun

🚊 3, 9, 19, 24, 50

Don't Miss

Oskar Schindler's Office

For many years after WWII, Oskar Schindler's old factory languished abandoned. Thankfully, Schindler's former office in the factory's administrative building survived that time intact. Here you'll see the names of the survivors and a symbolic 'Survivors' Ark' made of thousands of enamel pots similar to the ones made by Schindler's employees during the war.

Documentary Film

A thirty-minute introductory film features ordinary Kraków residents, including some of the former workers at the factory, who tell their own personalised (and often horrific) stories of life under the German Nazi occupation.

Audio/Visual Extravaganza

There's no one highlight here, rather the permanent exhibition is built around a series of rooms, each devoted to a specific theme, such as prewar Kraków, everyday life, the experience of Jewish residents, the resistance movement and the liberation of the city by the Soviet Union. Each theme is described with a mix of photos, period artefacts, radio broadcasts and old video to create an immersive experience.

Temporary Exhibitions

In addition to the permanent displays, the curators are committed to hosting thought-provoking and even occasionally controversial temporary shows within the overall theme of Kraków during WWII, such as the exhibition during our visit: 'Liberation or Subjugation? On the 70th Anniversary of the Battle for Kraków'.

AGNES KANTARUK/SHUTTERSTOCK ©

☑ Top Tips

▶ Admission is free on Mondays to the permanent exhibition, but get an early start because the number of people allowed in is limited.

▶ Note that on the first Monday of the month, the museum closes two hours early, at 2pm.

▶ Try to get to the museum well before closing, since the admission desk shuts down 90 minutes before closing.

▶ A good-value family admission ticket is available for 50zł (for two adults and two children up to 16 years of age).

▶ Leave at least two hours to take in fully the many audio and video presentations.

✗ Take a Break

Krako Slow Wines (p91), a little wine bar and restaurant, serves the best-value lunches near Schindler's Factory.

Local Life
Podgórze's Quirkier Side

Undoubtedly, Schindler's Factory and Plac Bohaterów Getta are the most visited attractions in Podgórze. But locals know that this neighbourhood on the edge has even more to offer, especially for travellers who are willing to wander off the beaten track.

1 Podgórze's Other Square

A world away from bleak Plac Bohaterów Getta, Podgórze's other square – the **Rynek Podgórsk** – is pleasant, green and integrated with the city in a way the district around Schindler's Factory is not. The square is dominated by the majestic **Church of St Joseph**. The neo-Gothic facade, from 1905, is festooned with gargoyles and crowned with a beautiful clock tower.

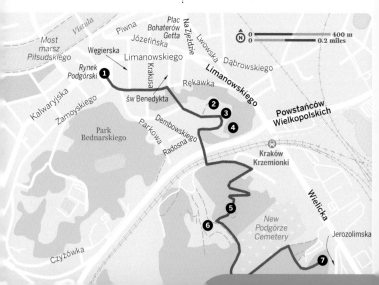

❷ Mysterious Church

Follow a footpath that leads up to the ancient **Church of St Benedict,** (Kościółek Św Benedykta; ul Rękawka, Lasota Hill; 🚌 3, 6, 9, 13, 23, 24, 50) one of the city's oldest and most mysterious churches. Historians are not certain of its origin, though archaeologists estimate that it dates from the 12th century. Although the interior has been restored, the church is only open once a year on the first Tuesday after Easter, when the spring festival of Rękawka is celebrated.

❸ Abandoned Fortress

Nearby is the abandoned **St Benedict Fort** (ul Rękawka, Lasota Hill; 🚌 3, 6, 9, 13, 23, 24, 50), which was built in the 1850s by the Austrians to defend the city from possible Russian or Prussian incursion from across the Vistula River. The interior is closed to visitors but you can still admire the two-story red-brick exterior, with its rounded artillery tower.

❹ Forgotten Cemetery

To the south is the **Old Podgórze Cemetery**, an 18th- and 19th-century burial ground that dates from the time when Podgórze was independent of the city of Kraków. The cemetery was ripped up by the Germans during WWII and today retains a wistful forgotten air.

❺ Pagan Mound

South of the cemetery, a footbridge crosses a busy highway, where a road leads up to a prehistoric pagan ritual site known as **Krakus Mound** (Kopiec Krakusa; ul Maryewskiego; ☉ dawn-dusk; 🚌 3, 6, 9, 13, 23, 24, 50). Nobody knows the exact origins of the 16m mound, but according to legend, it was the burial site of the city's founder, Prince Krak. Excavations in the 1930s could not confirm this story, but they did discover artefacts dating back to the 8th century.

❻ Creepy Quarry

Fans of the film *Schindler's List* will find the **Liban Quarry** (ul Za Torem; ☉ dawn-dusk; 🚌 3, 6, 9, 13, 23, 24, 50) especially fascinating. Director Steven Spielberg used this overgrown, long-abandoned quarry as the set for the Płaszów Labour Camp – and indeed some of the old movie props are still standing. The quarry was once a thriving Jewish-owned business but was taken over by the German Nazis during WWII, then let go to seed after the war (until Spielberg discovered its filmic potential).

❼ Forgotten Concentration Camp

Follow the footpath around the edge of the quarry and make your way to the unkempt grounds of the real **Płaszów Labour Camp** (ul Jerozolimska; ☉ dawn-dusk; 🚌 3, 6, 13, 23, 24, 50, 69). This forced-labour camp was built by occupying Germans during WWII to facilitate the liquidation of the nearby Podgórze ghetto. At its terrible height in 1943–44, the camp held some 25,000 people. These days, almost nothing of the camp survives.

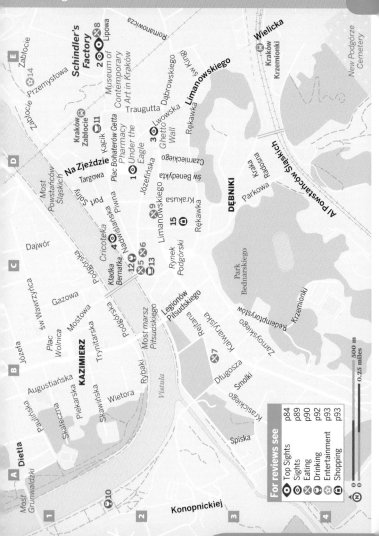

Zabłocie
Przemysłowa
© 14
Zabłocie

Romanowicza

Lipowa
Schindler's
Factory
2 © X 8

Museum of
Contemporary
Art in Kraków

Wielicka
Kraków
Krzemionki

New Podgórze
Cemetery

św Kingi

Dąbrowskiego
Limanowskiego

Traugutta

Lwowska
Ghetto
Wall
3 ●

Rękawka

Kraków
Zabłocie
Kącik
11
1 ● Under the
Eagle
Pharmacy
Plac Bohaterów Getta

Czarnieckiego

Na Zjeździe
Targowa

Józefińska

św Benedykta
Krakusa

Rękawka

DĘBNIKI
Parkowa

Al Powstańców Śląskich

Krępa
Radosna

Most
Powstańców
Śląskich

Port Solny
Nadwiślańska
Piwna

Limanowskiego
9 X
15 ●

Rynek
Podgórski

Park
Bednarskiego

Krzemionki

Cricoteka
Kładka
Bernatka
4 ●
12 ● X 5 X 6
13 ●

Dajwór

Podgórska

Gazowa

św Wawrzyńca

Mostowa

Trynitarska

Piekarska

Podgórska

Legionów
Piłsudskiego
Most marsz
Piłsudskiego

Kalwaryjska
Reitana

Redemptorystów
Zamoyskiego

Plac
Wolnica

KAZIMIERZ

Augustiańska

Skałeczna

Skawińska

Wietora

Rybaki

Vistula

Długosza

Smolki

Krasickiego

Dietla
Paulińska
Józefa

Most
Grunwaldzki

Spiska

Konopnickiej

500 m
0.25 miles

For reviews see	
● Top Sights	p84
● Sights	p89
⊗ Eating	p90
▲ Drinking	p92
◆ Entertainment	p93
● Shopping	p93

MARTIN LINDSAY/ALAMY ©

Display at Pharmacy Under the Eagle

Sights

Pharmacy Under the Eagle

MUSEUM

1 ◎ Map p88, D2

On the south side of Plac Bohaterów Getta is this museum in a former pharmacy, which was run by the non-Jewish Tadeusz Pankiewicz during the German Nazi occupation. The interior has been restored to its wartime appearance and tells the story of the ghetto and the role of the pharmacy in its daily life. (Apteka Pod Orłem; ☑12 656 5625; www.mhk.pl; Plac Bohaterów Getta 18; adult/concession 10/8zł, free Mon; ◎9am-5pm Tue-Sun, 10am-2pm Mon; ⛒3, 9, 19, 24, 50)

Museum of Contemporary Art in Kraków

MUSEUM

2 ◎ Map p88, E2

Opened in 2011, the Museum of Contemporary Art in Kraków, or MOCAK as it's known for short, is a major museum of modern art, and the first such building in Poland to be constructed from scratch. As it's right next to Schindler's Factory, the two attractions can be combined for an absorbing day out. (MOCAK; ☑12 263 4000; www.mocak.pl; ul Lipowa 4; adult/concession 10/5zł, free Tue; ◎11am-7pm Tue-Sun; �🛈; ⛒3, 9, 19, 24, 50)

Podgórze's Heroes

Podgórze is home to at least two prominent non-Jews who risked their own lives to save Jewish people during the Holocaust.

The best known, of course, is Oskar Schindler, the heavy-drinking profiteer and antihero, whose story was told to millions through Thomas Keneally's book *Schindler's Ark* (1982), and later in Steven Spielberg's mega-hit film *Schindler's List* (1993).

Schindler originally saved the lives of Jews because he needed their cheap labour at his enamelware factory (p84), though he went on to use his connections and pay bribes to keep his employees from being shipped off to concentration camps.

Another 'righteous Gentile' was pharmacist Tadeusz Pankiewicz, who was allowed to operate the Pharmacy Under the Eagle (p89) in the ghetto until the final deportation. Pankiewicz dispensed medicines (often without charge), carried news from the outside world and even allowed use of the establishment as a safe house on occasion.

As it says in the Talmud (and is movingly quoted at the end of Spielberg's film), 'Whoever saves one life, saves the world entire'.

Ghetto Wall   MONUMENT

3 👁 Map p88, D2

Just south of Plac Bohaterów Getta are the remains of the wartime Jewish ghetto wall from WWII, with a plaque marking the site. (ul Lwowska 25-29; 🚌 3, 9, 19, 24, 50)

Cricoteka   MUSEUM

4 👁 Map p88, C2

This modern museum is dedicated to the life and work of avant-garde Polish dramaturge Tadeusz Kantor and his experimental theatre company, Cricot 2. Most of the exhibition is given over to the stage props and mannequins used in performances, the significance of which may be lost on non-Poles, but the space also houses happenings and theatre performances. Check the website. (☎ 12 442 7770; www.news.cricoteka.pl; ul Nadwiślańska 2-4; adult/concession 10/5zł; 🕑 11am-7pm Tue-Sun; 🚌 3, 9, 19, 24, 50)

Eating

ZaKładka
Food & Wine   BISTRO €€€

5 🍴 Map p88, C2

This Parisian-style bistro specialises in simple French cooking centred around veal, rabbit, fresh fish and mussels and is one of the best places in this part of town. Expect courteous but formal service as well as an excellent wine list, featuring bottles from around Europe. The simplicity of the presentation extends to the decor: beige walls, black tables and wooden floors. (☑ 12 442 7442; www.zakladkabistro.pl; ul Józefińska 2; mains 35-50zł; ⏰ noon-11pm; 🛜; 🚊 6, 13, 19, 23)

TAO Sushi & More   ASIAN €€

6 ✖ Map p88, C2

Bright, welcoming Asian restaurant, with a small garden out back that has a children's play area. The emphasis is Japanese cooking, with sushi, teriyaki and a selection of bento boxes. They also do very good Thai food, with lots of vegan and vegetarian options to choose from. (☑ 725 880 304; www.zensushi.pl; ul Józefińska 4; mains 30-45zł; ⏰ noon-11pm; 🛜 👶 ♿; 🚊 3, 6, 11, 23)

With Fire & Sword   POLISH €€€

7 ✖ Map p88, B3

Named after the historical novel by Henryk Sienkiewicz, this dark, atmospheric restaurant re-creates the Poland of yesteryear. The wood interior is made even more rustic with animal pelts and a roaring fire. The menu features well-researched old-time recipes, such as the succulent roasted pig that comes stuffed with fruit. (Ogniem i Mieczem; ☑ 12 656 2328; www.ogniemimieczem.pl; Plac Serkowskiego 7; mains 40zł; ⏰ noon-midnight Mon-Sat, to 10pm Sun; 🚊 8, 10, 11, 23)

Krako Slow Wines   INTERNATIONAL €

8 ✖ Map p88, E2

It's hard to accurately characterise this little wine bar and restaurant, which serves the best-value lunches within 100 metres of Schindler's Factory. The emphasis is clearly on the wine, and there's a small wine shop next door featuring bottles

🔍 Local Life
Zabłocie

The opening of Schindler's Factory in 2010 has spurred a cultural and economic rebirth of Zabłocie, the eastern, formerly heavily industrialised part of Podgórze. Old factories are being rehabbed and repurposed into design studios and startup labs. After you've seen Schindler's Factory and MOCAK, stroll around the area and pop in for coffee at one of several trendy restaurants that have opened to cater to this influx of creatives. **Coffee Cargo** (Map p88, E1; ☑ 604 576 339; www.coffeeproficiency.com; Przemysłowa 3; ⏰ 8am-6pm Tue-Sat; 🛜; 🚊 3, 9, 19, 24, 50), a third-wave roaster, occupies a former warehouse and plays up the steampunk theme big time. **BAL** (Map p88, E1; ☑ 734 411 733; Ślusarska 9, enter from Przemysłowa; ⏰ 8.30am-9pm; 🛜; 🚊 3, 9, 19, 24, 50), another cafe, is all white and light, with large, collaborative tables to appeal to the industrial design crowd.

from Armenia, Georgia, Israel and Macedonia. It also serves salads, grilled meats and good-value daily luncheon specials, such as goulash. (☏669 225 222; www.krakoslowwines.pl; Lipowa 6f; mains 10-20zł; ⏱10am-10pm; 🚋3, 9, 19, 24, 50)

Delecta
PIZZA €

9 🍴 Map p88, D2

There are not a huge number of restaurants in Podgórze, but there is pizza. Tasty pies come with all kinds of toppings: some are authentic while others are inventive (the Delecta speciality pizza features ham, bacon and corn kernels). The place goes all out for Italy, with its Tuscan-sun decor. (☏12 423 5001; www.restauracja-delecta.pl; ul Limanowskiego 11; mains 17-24zł; ⏱11am-10pm Sun-Thu, to 11pm Fri & Sat; 🚋3, 9, 19, 24, 50)

Drinking

Forum Przestrzenie
BAR

10 🍺 Map p88, A2

In a highly creative re-use of an old communist-era eyesore, the Hotel Forum has been repurposed as a trendy, retro coffee and cocktail bar – and occasional venue for DJs, live music and happenings. In warm weather, lounge chairs are spread out over a patio overlooking the river. (☏514 342 939; www.forumprzestrzenie.com; ul Konopnickiej 28; ⏱10am-2am; 🛜; 🚋11, 18, 22, 52)

Kącik 6
CAFE

11 🍺 Map p88, D2

This tiny, family-run cafe is handy for a stop on the walk to or from Schindler's Factory. While it's mainly a cafe offering coffee and drinks, there's also a small eclectic food menu, featuring wraps, burgers, baked potatoes and homemade breads. There's a small garden out back and a side room for kids to play in. (☏602 761 054; ul Kącik 6; ⏱10am-10pm; 🛜🚻; 🚋3, 9, 19, 24, 50)

Cawa
CAFE, WINE BAR

Located next to Drukarnia (see 12 🍺 Map p88, C2), Cawa is a chic little wine bar, complete with post-industrial decor and spiffy waitstaff. Come for cappuccino or cava. If you're hungry, there are sophisticated, Med-style tapas listed on the slate board. (☏12 656 7456; www.cawacafe.pl; ul Nadwiślańska 1; ⏱8.30am-9.30pm Sun-Thu, to midnight Fri & Sat; 🛜; 🚋6, 13, 19, 23)

Drukarnia
CLUB

12 🍺 Map p88, C2

Old typewriters and newsprint wallpaper evoke the namesake 'print house', creating an arty atmosphere at this riverside venue. Upstairs, there are two spacious bars and pavement seating; downstairs is where the music goes down (jam sessions on Tuesday evenings, dance parties on Friday and Saturday). (☏12 656 6560; www.drukarnia-club.pl; ul Nadwiślańska 1; ⏱10am-last guest; 🛜; 🚋6, 13, 19, 23)

Cafe Rękawka
CAFE

13 Map p88, C2

The smell of fresh-brewed java and the sounds of jazz music entice you into this sweet sanctuary. It's a funny mismatch of burlap coffee bags, lace curtains and leafy plants, creating the perfect atmosphere to sink into a comfortable armchair and warm up with a cuppa. (☑12 296 2002; ul Brodzinskiego 4b; ⏰8am-7pm; 🛜; 🚊6, 13, 19, 23)

Entertainment

Fabryka Klub
LIVE MUSIC

14 Map p88, E1

This former factory in Podgórze has become the city's leading venue for indie and experimental live music. Shows vary from metal to electronica and are held in the hulking main hall of the plant or on the lawn. For concert info and tickets, check **TicketPro** (www.ticketpro.pl). Plenty of tables in warm weather and it's also great just for drinks. (☑530 053 551; Zabłocie 23; 🚊3, 9, 19, 24, 50)

Shopping

Starmach Gallery
GALLERY

15 Map p88, C2

Starmach is among the city's most prestigious galleries of contemporary painting and sculpture, exhibiting both emerging and established Polish artists. The modern gallery is housed in the former Jewish Zucher prayer house, a 19th-century neo-Gothic brick beauty. (☑12 656 4317; www.starmach.com.pl; ul Węgierska 5, Podgórze; ⏰11am-6pm Mon-Fri; 🚊3, 6, 11, 23)

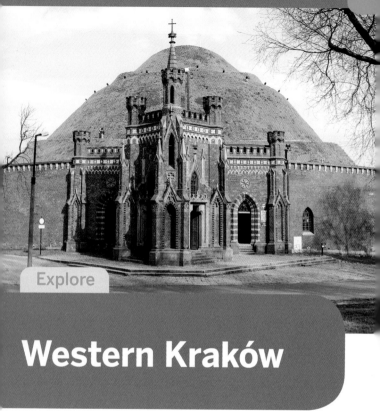

Explore

Western Kraków

Wander west of the Old Town and you'll discover Kraków at its most artistic and most verdant. This area was developed at the end of the 19th century, when Kraków was infused with Art Nouveau. To the west, the woodsy suburb of Zwierzyniec is the site of two monumental mounds that offer wonderful views. At the city's edge, the 485-hectare Wolski Forest is a perfect retreat for hikers, bikers, animal-lovers and monks.

AGNES KANTARUK/SHUTTERSTOCK ©

The Sights in a Day

☼ Choose comfortable shoes, since for the morning and afternoon at least, there's going to be a lot of walking. Start off with a fortifying breakfast under the trees at **Meho Cafe** (p102) and then make your way west via tram 1, 2 or 6 to stop Salvator, and continue on foot to the **Kościuszko Mound** (pictured left; p98) and its commanding views over Kraków.

☼ From here, find the footpaths and continue walking west about 3km to Las Wolski (see boxed text, p101), home of the **Zoological Gardens** (p99). If you're in the mood to walk some more, it's possible to hike to the quieter and more remote **Piłsudski Mound** (p98) or to visit the impressive fortress/church of the **Camaldolese Monks** (p99). If you'd rather do something indoors, return to the centre and take in the Gallery of 20th-Century Polish Painting at the main building of the **National Museum** (p98).

☾ For the evening, dress up and enjoy some classical music at the **Filharmonia Krakowska** (p103). If you're looking for something less fancy, relish in some well-executed Asian fusion food at **Restauracja Pod Norenami** (p101) or relax in the garden at **Dynia** (p101), then spend the night over microbrews at **CK Browar** (p102).

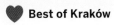 **Best of Kraków**

Food
Restauracja Pod Norenami (p101)

Music
Filharmonia Krakowska (p103)

Art
National Museum (p98)

With Kids
Hiflyer Balon Widokowy (p100)

Zoological Gardens (p99)

Shopping
Massolit Books & Cafe (p103)

Stary Kleparz (p103)

Getting There

🚋 **Trams** 4, 8, 13, 14 and 24 head west along ul Karmelicka.

🚋 **Trams** 1, 2 and 6 follow the Vistula westward to an important bus connection at Salwator.

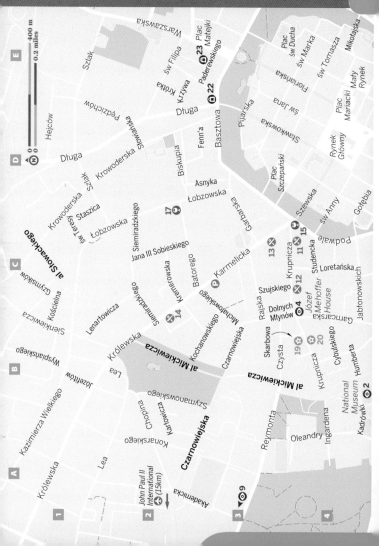

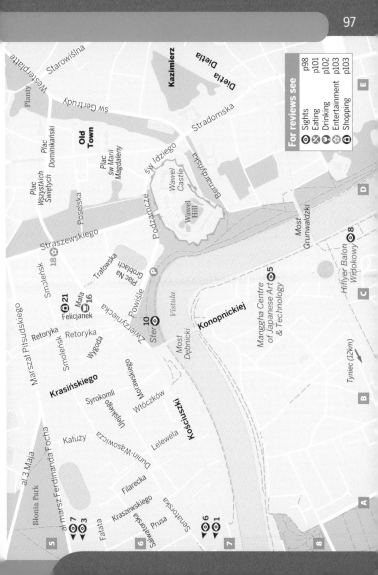

Starowiślna

Wesełe piątek

Planty

Kazimierz

Dietla

Dietla

Św Gertrudy

Old Town

Stradomska

Plac Dominikański

Plac św Marii Magdaleny

Plac Wszystkich Świętych

Poselska

Św Idziego

Bernardyńska

Straszewskiego

Smoleńsk

18 🏛

Wawel Castle

Wawel Hill

Podzamcze

Most Grunwaldzki

Trnacka

Plac Na Groblach

21 🍴

Mała Felicjanek

16 🍴

Smoleńsk

Retoryka

Retoryka

Wygoda

Zwierzyniecka

Powiśle

Ster

10 ⊙

Vistula

Most Dębnicki

Konopnickiej

Hflyer Balon Widokowy ⊙ 8

Manggha Centre of Japanese Art & Technology ⊙ 5

Tyniec (12km)

Marszał Piłsudskiego

Krasińskiego

Syrokomli

Ujejskiego

Morawskiego

Włóczków

Lelewela

Kościuszki

Dunin-Wąsowicza

Kałuży

al 3 Maja

al marsz Ferdinanda Focha

Fałata

Filarecka

Kraszewskiego

Senatorska

Śmiałowska

Prusa

Błonia Park

7 ⊙
3 ⊙

6 ⊙
1 ⊙

Sights

Kościuszko Mound MONUMENT

1 ⊙ Map p96, A7

The mound, dedicated to Polish (and American) military hero Tadeusz Kościuszko, was erected between 1820 and 1823, soon after the great man's death. The mound stands 34m high, and soil from the Polish and American battlefields where Kościuszko fought was placed here. The views over the city are spectacular. The memorial is located in the suburb of Zwierzyniec, just under 3km west of the Old Town. (Kopiec Kościuszki; ☑12 425 1116; www.kopieckosciuszki.pl; Al Waszyngtona 1; adult/concession 12/10zł; ⊙9am-dusk; 🚌1, 2, 6)

National Museum MUSEUM

2 ⊙ Map p96, B4

Three permanent exhibitions – the Gallery of 20th-Century Polish Painting, the Gallery of Decorative Art, and Polish Arms and National Colours – are housed in this main branch of the National Museum in Kraków, 500m west of the Old Town down ul Piłsudskiego. The most notable collection is the painting gallery, which houses an extensive collection of Polish painting (and some sculpture) covering the period from 1890 until the present day. (Muzeum Narodowe w Krakowie; ☑12 433 5540; www.muzeum.krakow.pl; Al 3 Maja 1; adult/concession 28/19zł, free Sun; ⊙10am-6pm Tue-Sat, to 4pm Sun; 🚌20)

Piłsudski Mound MONUMENT

3 ⊙ Map p96, A5

This mound-based memorial was erected in honour of Marshal Józef Piłsudski after his death in 1935; it was formed from soil taken from WWI Polish battle sites. The views of the city are excellent. Bus 134, which terminates at the zoo, is the nearest public transport. You can also reach the mound from the Kościuszko Mound on foot via a well-marked trail, taking about 2½ hours. (Kopiec Piłsudskiego w Krakowie; admission free; ⊙24hr; 🚌134)

Józef Mehoffer House MUSEUM

4 ⊙ Map p96, C4

The 'Young Poland' artist lived in this stately home from 1932 until his death in 1946. The museum preserves the elegant interiors, with many original furnishings and artwork. Look out for work by the artist, including stained-glass windows and portraits of his wife. Be sure not to miss the lovely garden. (Dom Józefa Mehoffera; ☑12 433 5889; www.mnk.pl; ul Krupnicza 26; adult/concession 9/5zł, Sun free; ⊙10am-4pm Tue-Sun; 🚌2, 4, 8, 13, 14, 18, 20, 24)

Manggha Centre of Japanese Art & Technology MUSEUM

5 ⊙ Map p96, C7

This museum is the brainchild of Polish film director Andrzej Wajda, who donated the Kyoto Prize money he received in 1987 to fund a permanent

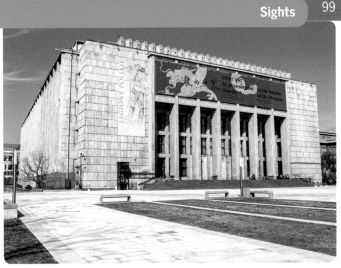

National Museum

home for the National Museum's extensive collection of Japanese art, ceramics and scrolls. The bulk of the collection is made up of several thousand pieces assembled by Feliks Jasieński (1861–1929), an avid traveller and essayist, known as Mangha. Note the location is across the river from the Old Town. (✆12 267 2703; www.manggha.pl; ul Konopnickiej 26; adult/concession 20/15zł, free Tue; ⊙10am-6pm Tue-Sun; ⊒11, 18, 22, 52)

Monastery of Camaldolese Monks ARCHITECTURE

6 ◉ Map p96, A7

The Monastery of Camaldolese Monks sits atop Silver Mountain, overlooking the Vistula River, in an outlying suburb west of the Old Town. It's well worth a few hours to visit. Men can visit the church and crypt any day from 8am to 11am and 3pm to 4.30pm. Women can enter only on certain feast days, including Easter, Easter Monday, the second and fourth Sundays in July, Assumption of Mary (15 August), and Christmas. (Klasztor Kamedułów; www.kameduli.info; Srebrna Góra, Western Kraków; ⊙8-11am & 3-4.30pm; ⊒1,2, 6)

Zoological Gardens ZOO

7 ◉ Map p96, A5

The 20-hectare zoological gardens are well-tended and home to about 1500 animals. Highlights include a pair of Indian elephants, pygmy

Understand

'Remember You Must Die'

'Memento Mori' is the motto of the reclusive Camaldolese monks (p99). Just to make sure they live by this motto, the monks keep the skulls of their predecessors in their hermitages. It's just one of many practices that have earned this ancient order a reputation for asceticism and austerity.

Part of the Benedictine family, the Camaldolese order came to Poland from Italy in 1603. Kraków was the first of the Camaldolese seats in Poland; a church and 20 hermitages were established here between 1603 and 1642, and the whole complex was walled in. Not much has changed since.

Opposite the entrance to the monastery is the massive white limestone facade of the church. Underneath the chancel of the church is the crypt of the hermits. Bodies are placed into niches without coffins and sealed. Latin inscriptions state the age of the deceased and period spent in the hermitage. The niches are opened after 80 years and the remains moved to a place of permanent rest. It's then the hermits take the skulls to keep them company in their shelters.

hippopotamuses, and a herd of rare Asian horses (Przewalski) that once roamed the Mongolian steppes. Bus 134 heads to the zoo from its terminus near the National Museum. (Ogród Zoologiczny; 12 425 3551; www.zoo-krakow.pl; Al Kasy Oszczędności Miasta Krakowa 14; adult/concession 18/10zł; 9am-6pm; 134)

Hiflyer Balon Widokowy

BALLOONING

8 Map p96, D8

For fabulous views of Wawel Castle and the Old Town, it's hard to beat the Hiflyer hot-air balloon. Moored along the Vistula River, near the Grunwald Bridge, across the river from Kazimierz, the enormous balloon takes passengers for a 15-minute float 150m over the city. On a clear day you can see the Tatras. (Hiflyer Viewing Balloon; 511 802 202; www.hiflyer.pl; Bulwar Wołyński; adult/concession 42/34zł; 10am-8pm Apr-Sep; 18, 19, 22)

Wisła Kraków

SPECTATOR SPORTS

9 Map p96, A3

Poland's most successful football club, Wisła Kraków, has won several Polish championships in the past decade. It is particularly strong in its home stadium. (tickets 12 623 9595; www.wisla.krakow.pl; ul Reymonta 20; box office 10am-7pm Mon-Fri, 10am-4pm Sat & Sun; 20)

Ster

CRUISE

10 Map p96, C6

River cruises around the city or as far as Tyniec Abbey aboard the *Sobieski*, berthed not far from the

Dębnicki Bridge, below the Sheraton Kraków hotel and accessed from ul Zwierzyniecka. The trip allows a one-hour stop at the abbey before turning around. Reserve tickets online or by phone. (Vistula Shipping Centre; ☎601 560 250; www.ster.net.pl; adult/concession 1hr 20/15zł, 3hr 50/35zł; ⏰10am-6pm May-Oct; 🚊1, 2, 6)

Eating

Restauracja Pod Norenami
ASIAN, VEGETARIAN €€

11 ✕ Map p96, C4

This warm and inviting Asian-fusion restaurant is ideal for vegans and vegetarians. The menu pivots from Japanese to Thai and Vietnamese, with lots of spicy noodle and rice dishes, vegetarian sushi and many other choices. Breakfast (served from 10am to noon) has Middle Eastern overtones, with hummus and pita and spicy scrambled eggs. Book in advance. (☎661 219 289; www.podnorenami.pl; ul Krupnicza 6; mains 18-30zł; ⏰10am-10pm; 🛜🗗; 🚊2, 4, 8, 13, 14, 18, 20, 24)

Dynia
INTERNATIONAL €€

12 ✕ Map p96, C4

While Dynia's interior is chic – with leather furniture and avant-garde floral arrangements – it is the gorgeous, green courtyard that is the most enticing. Crumbling brick walls surround the fern-filled space, evoking an atmosphere of elegance amid decay. The menu is a modern European mix, with a few low-cal and vegetarian options on the salad menu. (☎12 430 0838; www.dynia.krakow.pl; ul Krupnicza 20; mains 25-40zł; ⏰8am-11pm Mon-Fri, 9am-11pm Sat & Sun; 🛜; 🚊2, 4, 8, 13, 14, 18, 20, 24)

Trattoria Mamma Mia
PIZZA €€

13 ✕ Map p96, C3

We know you didn't come to Poland to eat pizza, but if you have a craving, go for the delicious, crispy, thin-crusted pies that come out of the wood-burning oven at Mamma Mia. Also serves very good pasta, meat and fish dishes. (☎12 422 2868; www.mammamia.net.pl; ul Karmelicka 14; pizza 18 25zł, mains 25-40zł; ⏰8am-11pm Mon-Fri, 9am-11pm Sat & Sun; 🛜; 🚊4, 8, 13, 14, 24)

⊙ Local Life
Leafy Las Wolski

The 485-hectare Las Wolski (Wolski Forest), west of Zwierzyniec, is the largest forested area within the city limits. In addition to being home to the Zoological Gardens (p99) and Piłsudski Mound (p98), it's a popular picnic and weekend destination for city dwellers. A fun day out is to combine a visit here with the two sights mentioned above as well as to the nearby Kościuszko Mound.

Alebriche

MEXICAN €€

14 Map p96, B2

This simple, unadorned space may serve the most authentic Mexican food in Kraków. The emphasis here is not so much on modern mass Mexican fare, like tacos and burritos, but rather on old school items like tamales, served stuffed with poblano peppers and cheese, or with chicken in a mole sauce. They also serve traditional Mexican breakfasts. (⌖510 550 211; www.restauracjalebriche.com; ul Karmelicka 56; mains 20-35zł; ⏱10am-10pm; ⏺; ⛾4, 13, 14, 24)

Drinking

CK Browar

MICROBREWERY

15 Map p96, C4

Serious tipplers will head for this below-ground microbrewery with its cavernous drinking hall. The amber fluid is brewed on the spot to an old Austro-Hungarian recipe, then poured straight from the tanks into patrons' glasses. Beware the CK Dunkel brew, which is 7% alcohol. (⌖12 429 2505; www.ckbrowar.krakow.pl; ul Podwale 6/7; ⏱9am-1am; ⏺; ⛾2, 13, 18, 20)

Meho Cafe

CAFE

Located in the blooming garden of the Józef Mehoffer House (see 4 ⏺ Map p96, C4), Meho Cafe has a handful of tables which are carefully arranged around a leafy oak tree. (In case of rain, you can sit inside the cosy cafe.) Service is leisurely, so sit back and enjoy the delightful setting. In addition to coffee and tea, they also have an eclectic, light lunch menu of salads, tortillas and risottos. (⌖600 480 049; www.mehocafe.pl; ul Krupnicza 26; ⏱10am-8pm; ⛾2, 4, 8, 13, 14, 18, 20, 24)

Café Szafe

CAFE

16 Map p96, C5

The colourful cafe on the corner is a cupboard full of surprises, from the whimsical sculptured creatures lurking in the corners to the intriguing artwork that hangs on the walls. The place hosts concerts, films and other arty events. (⌖663 905 652; www.cafeszafe.com; ul Felicjanek 10; ⏱9am-1am Mon-Fri, 10am-midnight Sat & Sun; ⏺; ⛾1, 2, 6)

Sabor'33

CLUB

17 Map p96, D2

This Latino club reverberates to the sound of salsa, merengue, samba and bossa nova. There are themed nights through the week, like the popular Cuba Havana party, as well as dance lessons. (⌖12 423 4470; www.sabor33krakow.weebly.com; ul Batorego 1; ⏱8pm-3am Tue-Sat; ⛾4, 8, 13, 14, 24)

Entertainment

Filharmonia Krakowska
CLASSICAL MUSIC

18 ⭐ Map p96, C5

This concert hall is home to one of the best orchestras in the country. (Filharmonia im. Karola Szymanowskiego w Krakowie; ☎ reservations 12 619 8722, tickets 12 619 8733; www.filharmonia.krakow.pl; ul Zwierzyniecka 1; ⏱ box office 10am-2pm & 3-7pm Tue-Fri; 🚊 1, 2, 6)

Teatr Groteska
THEATRE

19 ⭐ Map p96, B4

The 'Grotesque Theatre' stages mostly puppet shows and is well worth a visit. It's 450m west of the Planty along ul Krupnicza. Note the troupe takes an annual summer break in July and August. (☎ 12 633 4822; www. groteska.pl; ul Skarbowa 2; ⏱ box office 8am-noon & 3-5pm Mon-Fri; 🚊 2, 4, 8, 13, 14, 18, 20, 24)

Kino Paradox
CINEMA

20 ⭐ Map p96, B4

This popular art-house cinema features independent European, Polish and international films that will likely never make it to the multiplex. (☎ 12 430 0015; www.kinoparadox. pl; Centrum Młodzieży im H Jordana, ul Krupnicza 38; tickets 10-12zł; 🚊 2, 4, 8, 13, 14, 18, 20, 24)

Shopping

Massolit Books & Cafe
BOOKS

21 🔒 Map p96, C5

Highly atmospheric book emporium selling English-language fiction and nonfiction, both new and secondhand. The collection is particularly strong on Polish and Central European authors in translation. There's also a cafe area with loads of character. (☎ 12 432 4150; www. massolit.com; ul Felicjanek 4; ⏱ 10am-8pm Sun-Thu, 10am-9pm Fri & Sat; 🛜; 🚊 1, 2, 6)

Księgarnia Pod Globusem
BOOKS

22 🔒 Map p96, E3

This 'bookstore under the globe' carries a great selection of maps and travel guides. Look for the green copper globe perched atop the steeple of the amazing Art Nouveau building. (☎ 12 422 1739; www.liberglob.pl; ul Długa 1; ⏱ 10am-7pm Mon-Fri, to 2pm Sat; 🚊 2, 4, 14, 19, 20, 24)

Stary Kleparz
MARKET

23 🔒 Map p96, E3

This sprawling covered market dates back to the 12th century and is the city's most atmospheric place to shop for fresh fruits, vegetables and flowers. You'll also find meats, cheeses, spices and bread, as well as clothes. (☎ 12 634 1532; www.starykleparz.com; ul Paderewskiego, Rynek Kleparski; ⏱ 6am-6pm Mon-Fri, to 4pm Sat, 8am-3pm Sun; 🛜; 🚊 2, 4, 14, 19, 20, 24)

Explore

Eastern Kraków

Kraków Główny Train Station is the first port of call for most visitors to Kraków. From here, they beat a hasty retreat into the Old Town, only to emerge a few days later to board their train out of town. Many never experience Kraków outside the Planty, yet this part of the city pulses to a different beat. It is here that Kraków loses its aura of medieval magic and holiday haven, and takes on the rhythms of the workaday world.

The Sights in a Day

☀️ Start out with a hearty Polish breakfast at **Klimaty Południa** (p110) and then head over to the open-air market **Hala Targowa** (p111) to pick over some of the antiques and (frankly) junk on display. Spend the rest of the morning, depending on your interests, strolling through the **Botanical Gardens** (p107) or marvelling at the **New Jewish Cemetery** (p108).

☀️ At midday, grab a cheap, filling and delicious lunch at one of our favourite veggie joints, **Glonojad** (p108). Spend the rest of the afternoon poking around impressive Plac Matejki, taking in the **Grunwald Monument** (pictured left; p108) and **St Florian's Church** (p107). If you happen to catch a hot day, repair to the pool and water-based fun at **Park Wodny** (p139).

🌙 For the evening, start off with an Italian meal on the terrace at hidden **Il Calzone** (p110), followed by a night of classical opera at the city's futuristic opera house **Opera Krakowska** (p110). Or, if you're travelling with children and the idea of an opera sounds like a snooze (at least for them), check out Europe's biggest IMAX cinema screen at **IMAX Cinema City** (p110).

 **Best of Kraków**

Food
Glonojad (p108)

Music
Opera Krakowska (p110)

With Kids
Park Wodny (p139)

Shopping
Hala Targowa (p111)

Jewish Heritage
New Jewish Cemetery (p108)

Getting There

🚋 **Trams** 2, 3, 4, 10, 14, 19, 24 and 52 serve the Kraków Główny train station and the Galeria Krakowska shopping centre.

🚋 **Trams** 1, 14 and 22 are useful for points further east, including the Kraków Plaza.

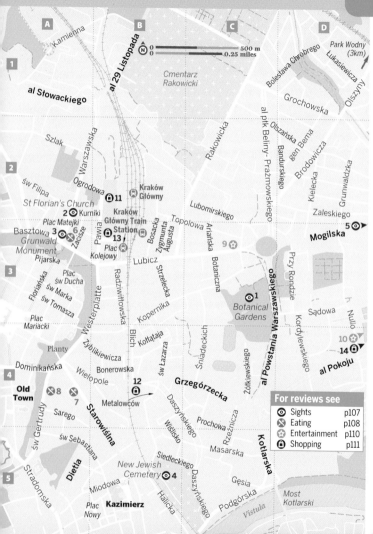

Park Wodny
(3km)

500 m
0.25 miles

Cmentarz
Rakowicki

al Słowackiego

al 29 Listopada

Bolesława Chróbrego

Łukasiewicza

Olszyny

Grochowska

Kamienna

Szlak

Warszawska

Ogrodowa

św Filipa

St Florian's Church

**Kraków
Główny**

🔒 11

2 ◎ Kurniki

**Kraków
Główny Train
Station**

13 🚈

Plac
Kolejowy

Plac Matejki

Basztowa 3 ◎ 6 Zacisze

Grunwald
Monument

Pijarska

Rakowicka

al płk Beliny-Prazmowskiego

Olszańska

gen Bema

Bandurskiego

Brodowicza

Kielecka

Grunwaldzka

Zaleskiego

5 ◎▶

Mogilska

Lubomirskiego

Topolowa

Ariańska

Bosacka

Pawia

Zygmunta
Augusta

Strzelecka

Botaniczna

9 ☆

◎ 1
**Botanical
Gardens**

Przy Rondzie

al Powstania Warszawskiego

Sądowa

Nullo

Kordylewskiego

10 ☆▶

14 🔒▶

al Pokoju

Lubicz

Florjańska

Plac
św Ducha

św Marka

św Tomasza

Plac
Mariacki

Planty

Dominikańska

Westerplatte

Radziwiłłowska

Kopernika

Blich

Kołłątaja

Żyblikiewicza

Bonerowska

Wielopole

12

Metalowców

Sniadeckich

św Łazarza

Grzegórzecka

Żółkiewskiego

Daszyńskiego

Prochowa

Rzeźnicza

Kotlarska

**Old
Town**

◎ 8 ◎
7

Sarego

Starowiślna

Dietla

św Sebastiana

Stradomska

Wiślisko

Siedleckiego

Daszyńskiego

Masarska

**New Jewish
Cemetery** ◎ 4

Gęsia

Halicka

Podgórska

*Most
Kotlarski*

Vistula

Plac
Nowy

Kazimierz

Miodowa

św Gertrudy

For reviews see

◎ Sights   p107
◎ Eating   p108
☆ Entertainment   p110
🔒 Shopping   p111

BRASILAO/SHUTTERSTOCK ©

St Florian's Church

Sights

Botanical Gardens

GARDENS

1 ⊙ Map p106, C3

The botanical gardens of Jagiellonian University offer nearly ten hectares of green and flowery loveliness. The gardens offer exhibits of medicinal plants, endangered species of Polish flora and plants described in the Bible. The amazing orchid collection dates to the 1860s. (Ogród Botaniczny; ☎12 663 3635; www.ogrod.uj.edu.pl; ul Kopernika 27; adult/concession 7zł/4zł; ⊙garden 9am-7pm daily, greenhouses 10am-6pm Sat-Thu, museum 10am-2pm Wed & Fri, 11am-3pm Sat; 🚊4, 5, 10, 14, 20, 52)

St Florian's Church

CHURCH

2 ⊙ Map p106, A2

This 12th-century church's location was chosen by the oxen that carried the remains of St Florian from Rome. When the beasts would go no further, it was interpreted as a sign of a holy site. In 1582, the church survived a fire that swept through the city; since then, St Florian has been a patron saint of Kraków and firefighters. (Kościół Św Floriana; ☎12 422 4842; www.swflorian.net; ul Warszawska 1b; ⊙6am-7pm; 🚊2, 3, 4, 14, 19, 20, 24)

Grunwald Monument MONUMENT

3 ⊙ Map p106, A3

This imposing monument celebrates the epic 1410 Battle of Grunwald, when a joint army of Poles and Lithuanians defeated the Teutonic Knights. This statue is a copy from the mid-1970s, based on an original from 1910 that was destroyed by the Nazis during WWII. (Plac Matejki; 🚊2, 4, 14, 19, 20, 24)

Understand

The 'New' Jewish Cemetery

Strolling through Kraków's lively streets, the Holocaust and the tragedy of WWII for the Jewish people can feel far away. This forgotten cemetery, located in a remote part of eastern Kraków beyond a train underpass, retains something of the sadness of those days. The Nazis made short work of the cemetery during the war and used many of the grave markers as paving stones and scrap. It's touching to see how much effort has gone into trying to restore the cemetery and rescue the remnants that could be recovered.

Though the cemetery has an undeniably spooky feel, it's also very peaceful and something of a refuge from the busy city. Men should remember to cover their heads on entering.

New Jewish Cemetery CEMETERY

4 ⊙ Map p106, B5

Although it's the 'new' Jewish cemetery, it was established as early as 1800. Though many of the grave markers were destroyed during the Holocaust, some 9000 tombstones are visible. Many of these have eerie and elaborate carvings. (Nowy Cmentarz Żidowsky; ul Miodowa 55; ⊙9am-6pm Sun-Thu; 🚊3, 9, 19, 24, 50)

Polish Aviation Museum MUSEUM

5 ⊙ Map p106, D3

Old aircraft, engines and other aviation equipment exhibited on the grounds of one Europe's oldest military airports, that traces its roots to the days of the Austro-Hungarian Empire. (✆12 642 8700; www.muzeumlotnictwa.pl; al Jana Pawła II 39; adult/concession 14/7zł, Tue free; ⊙9am-5pm Tue-Sun; 🚊4, 5, 9, 10, 52)

Eating

Glonojad VEGETARIAN €

6 ✖ Map p106, A3

Attractive modern vegetarian restaurant with a great view onto Plac Matejki, just north of the Barbican. The diverse menu has a variety of tasty dishes including samosas, curries, potato pancakes, burritos, gnocchi and soups. There's also an

Understand

Kraków Under Communism

While the city, particularly the centre, doesn't look like a place that suffered long under communism, Kraków – along with the rest of Poland – spent four long decades under the thumb of the Soviet Union and its local allies, the Polish United Workers' Party.

'Liberated' by the Soviet Union

There had been far-left and communist parties operating in Poland since the start of the 20th century, but communism only got a foothold in Poland after the end of WWII and the German Nazi occupation, when the country was 'liberated' by Soviet troops in the spring of 1945.

At the Yalta Conference, the three Allied leaders, US President Franklin Roosevelt, British Prime Minister Winston Churchill and Soviet leader Josef Stalin, fatefully agreed to leave Poland within the Soviet domain. Stalin moved quickly to implement an intensive Sovietisation campaign: wartime resistance leaders were charged with Nazi collaboration and executed, and the Polish United Workers' Party took over the government.

Proletariat Kraków

Kraków became the target of special attention due to its traditional intellectual and spiritual bent. In 1949, the Polish authorities, under the instruction of the Soviet Union, created the planned workers' community of Nowa Huta (see the Local Life feature, p112), complete with a giant steel mill and utopian social structures. The point was to stick a finger in the eye of aristocratic Kraków.

Ironically, the steelworkers would cause continuous problems for the communist regime – protesting the prohibition of a local church and attempting to blow up a statue of Lenin that once stood in Nowa Huta's main square, Plac Centralny.

Solidarity Foothold

Significantly, Nowa Huta became a stronghold for Solidarity, the labour movement that would eventually bring down the communist regime. In 1978 the archbishop of Kraków, Karol Wojtyła, was elected as the first Polish pontiff, taking the name Pope John Paul II.

The pope's triumphal visit to his homeland the following year inspired his Catholic compatriots and dramatically increased the political ferment. According to recent polls, nearly three-quarters of Poles credit Pope John Paul II with the liberation of Poland in 1989.

all-day breakfast menu, so there's no need to jump out of that hotel bed too early. (📞12 346 1677; www.glonojad.com; Plac Matejki 2; mains 16-20zł; ⏰8am-10pm; 📶♿; 🚌2, 4, 14, 19, 20, 24)

Il Calzone
ITALIAN €€

7 🍴 Map p106, A4

This pleasant slice of Italy is a well-kept secret, tucked away in a quiet nook set back from the street next to the Hotel Pugetów. Pleasant white-washed decor, charming outdoor terrace, and the food is excellent value. (📞12 429 5141; www.ilcalzone.pl; ul Starowiślna 15a; mains 30-45zł; ⏰noon-11pm Mon-Thu; 📶; 🚌1, 3, 19, 24, 52)

Klimaty Południa
INTERNATIONAL €€

8 🍴 Map p106, A4

Wander away from the busy street, through the courtyard, to this hidden gem. The menu is vaguely

---

🔍 Local Life
Late Night Sausage Stand

The Hala Targowa (p111) is home to one the city's most famous late-night sausage stands, and after a night of carousing you can bet that more than a few locals will make their way here for a well-earned snack before bed. The grilling begins at 8pm nightly (except Sunday) and runs till about 3am. Look for two guys huddled over an open fire next to an old van (often with a long queue).

Mediterranean, though Polish and other influences are evident. A good wine list and cosy quarters – and very good breakfasts – make it an excellent stop. Book a table online, as seating is limited. (📞12 422 0357; www.klimatypoludnia.pl; ul Św Gertrudy 5; mains 25-40zł; ⏰9am-midnight; 📶; 🚌6, 8, 10, 13, 18)

Entertainment

Opera Krakowska
OPERA

9 ⭐ Map p106, C3

The Kraków Opera performs in the strikingly modern red building at the Mogilskie roundabout. The setting is decidedly 21st century, but the repertoire spans the ages, incorporating everything from Verdi to Bernstein. (📞12 296 6260; www.opera.krakow.pl; ul Lubicz 48; tickets 20-200zł; ⏰10am-7pm Mon-Fri, or two hours before performances at box office; 🚌4, 10, 14, 20, 52)

IMAX Cinema City
CINEMA

10 ⭐ Map p106, D4

The great thing about IMAX theatres is that you don't need to understand the words to appreciate the incredible cinematography surrounding you. Some of the nature films are 3D, which means you might actually feel that snapping turtle nip you on the nose. (📞12 290 9090; www.cinema-city.pl; al Pokoju 44, Kraków Plaza; adult/concession 34/23zł; 📶; 🚌1, 14, 22)

Shopping

Galeria Krakowska
SHOPPING CENTRE

11 🔒 Map p106, B2

In case there was any question about Poland transitioning to capitalism, here's your answer. The massive mall near the train station contains 270 stores; of interest to world-weary travellers are the food court and American bookstore. (📞12 428 9900; ul Pawia 5; ⏱9am-10pm Mon-Sat, 10am-9pm Sun; 🚊2, 3, 4, 10, 14, 19, 24, 52)

Hala Targowa
MARKET

12 🔒 Map p106, B4

An outdoor flea market, where you'll find lots of old books with yellowed pages, postcards depicting the Kraków of yesteryear, paintings and icons, and loads of other trash and treasure. Vendors set up here daily but Sunday before noon is best. There's also a popular sausage stand here for late-night street food (8pm to 3am Monday to Friday). (ul Grzegórzecka 3; ⏱7am-3pm; 🚊1, 9, 11, 22, 50)

Empik
BOOKS

13 🔒 Map p106, B3

Big chain bookshop, also good for maps, newspapers, magazines and hard-to-find Polish films on DVD to take back home. This branch, on the first floor of the Galeria Krakowska

Galeria Krakowska

shopping centre, has arguably the best selection. (📞22 451 0385; www.empik.com; ul Pawia 5; ⏱9.30am-9pm; 🚊2, 3, 4, 10, 14, 19, 24, 52)

Kraków Plaza
SHOPPING CENTRE

14 🔒 Map p106, D4

Handy shopping centre if you happen to be staying out this direction. In addition to a Carrefour supermarket for picking up food, there are lots of boutiques, including a Zara. This is also home to Poland's – and apparently Europe's – biggest IMAX cinema screen. (📞12 684 1600; www.krakowplaza.pl; al Pokoju 44; ⏱10am-9pm Mon-Sat, to 8pm Sun; 📶; 🚊1, 14, 22)

Local Life
Workers' Paradise in Nowa Huta

A special gift from 'Uncle Joe' Stalin, the suburb of Nowa Huta ('New Steel-works') consisted of a massive steel mill and a Socialist-Realist residential area. It's a perfectly preserved example of utopian, communist-era housing. Far greener than it ever was in its 1960s heyday (the steel mill has been greatly cleaned up), it's worth poking around to admire the grandiose scale and harmonious retro-futuristic architecture.

Getting There

Nowa Huta is 6km east of the Old Town

🚊 Tram 4 runs directly to Nowa Huta's Plac Centralny and the old Nowa Huta Steelworks; trams 10 and 16 run to the religious sites on ul Klasztorna

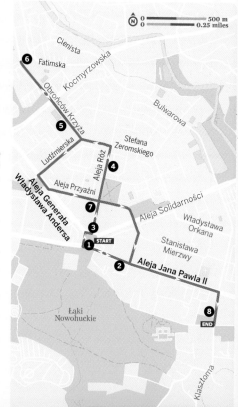

1 'Ronald Reagan Square'

Leave the tram at **Plac Centralny**. The square, built in 1949, was once named for Stalin and dotted by a statue of Lenin – and is now officially named after former US President Ronald Reagan.

2 Muzeum PRL-u

Take a peek inside the **Muzeum PRL-u** (☏12 446 7821; www.mprl.pl; os Centrum E1; adult/concession 6/4zł; ☺9am-5pm Mon-Fri; ⛟4, 10, 16, 21), a low-tech, work-in-progress museum dedicated to the quarter's communist past, located in the Socialist-Realist Światowid cinema. There's also an atomic fall-out shelter in the basement.

3 Alley of the Roses

Nowa Huta's central avenue is **Aleja Róż** (Alley of the Roses). It's a wide, elegant thoroughfare, where you can see the planners' intentions to glorify the lives of workers. Stop by **Cepelix** (☏12 644 1571; os Centrum B1; ☺10am-6pm Mon-Fri, to 1pm Sat; ⛟4, 10, 16), a souvenir shop that retains its original 1960s retro interior.

4 Nowa Huta Museum

North of Plac Centralny, the **Nowa Huta Museum** (☏12 425 9775; www.mhk. pl; os Słoneczne 16; adult/concession 6/4zł, free Wed; ☺9.30am-5pm Tue-Sun; ⛟4, 10, 16, 21) features well-curated displays of Nowa Huta's past, including on our visit a more-interesting-than-it-sounds exhibition on 19th-century Austrian forts.

5 Theatre for the People

The '50s and '60s were a period of architectural and theatrical experimentation. The **Teatr Ludowy** (People's Theatre; ☏12 680 2112; www.ludowy.pl; Osiedle Teatralne 34; ⛟4, 14, 15) achieved both, with a startling Socialist-Realist exterior and a daring repertoire of avant-garde productions.

6 Church for the Workers

Another example of architectural experimentation, the retro-modern **Arka Pana** (Lord's Ark; ☏12 644 0624; www. arkapana.pl; ul Obrońców Krzyża 1; ☺9am-6pm; ⛟1, 5) was the first church in Nowa Huta. It was built in 1977 after a campaign by the local bishop (Karol Wojtyła), as the quarter was originally planned to be free of churches.

7 Dining in 'Style'

Nowa Huta is short on dining options, but **Restauracja Stylowa** (☏12 644 2619; os Centrum C3; ☺9am-10pm; ⛟4, 14, 15) offers the prospect of a worker's lunch, amid the charmingly dated interior of what was once the area's most elegant eatery.

8 Before the Mills

Walk or take the tram east to ul Klasztorna, where two ecclesiastical sites beckon. The **Cistercian Abbey** (Opactwo Cystersów; ☏12 644 2331; www. mogila.cystersi.pl; ul Klasztorna 11; ☺9am-5pm; ⛟10, 16), from the year 1222, consists of a church and monastery with a large park behind it, while across the street, the wooden **Church of St Bartholomew** dates from the mid-15th century.

Top Sights
Auschwitz-Birkenau Memorial & Museum

Getting There

🚌 (12zł, 1½ hours, many daily) Buses drop you off in the parking lot opposite the entrance.

🚆 (14zł, 1½ hours, hourly) Trains drop you 1.5km from the museum entrance.

The Nazi Concentration and Extermination Camp of Auschwitz-Birkenau is synonymous with genocide and the Holocaust. More than a million Jews as well as many Poles and Roma were murdered here by German occupiers during WWII. Both sections of the camp, the main camp Auschwitz I and a much larger outlying camp at Birkenau (Auschwitz II), 2km away, have been preserved and are open for visitors. Make sure to leave yourself a full day to absorb what is a profound and moving experience.

Don't Miss

Auschwitz Main Gate
The tour begins in the visitors centre of the main camp with the screening of a graphic 17-minute documentary film on the liberation of the camp by Soviet soldiers in 1945. (The film is not recommended for children under 14.) The tour then proceeds through the infamous gates bearing the slogan 'Arbeit Macht Frei' (Work Sets You Free) to the main mustering point for the prisoners, where they would be called for morning roll and hear camp announcements.

Barracks Exhibitions
The bulk of the exhibits in the main camp are located in former barracks, with each building (a 'block') given a number and a specific theme, such as how the camp was created, the confiscation of personal property, daily life, and the resistance movement. Each block holds its own horrors, such as photos of those who were killed or the tiny bunks where dozens of prisoners were forced to sleep, but perhaps none is more starkly terrifying than the massive sea of human hair (in Block 4) that was collected and sold to make cloth.

Block 11 – The 'Death Block'
The tour proceeds through the blocks and lingers at Block 11, known as the notorious 'Death Block'. While most of the mass killings took place in Birkenau, it was here in this small courtyard where thousands of victims were lined up and shot in front of the Wall of Death. The basement contains cells where prisoners were tortured, held in solitary confinement and starved to death. At one end of the grounds, you can actually enter a gas chamber and crematoria.

DANIEL ALEXANDER/DESIGN PICS/GETTY IMAGES ©

📞 guides 33 844 8100

www.auschwitz.org

ul Więźniów Oświęcimia 20

tours adult/concession 40/30zł

🕐 8am-7pm Jun-Aug, to 6pm Apr-May, to 5pm Mar & Sep, to 4pm Feb & Oct, to 3pm Jan & Nov, to 2pm Dec

☑ Top Tips

▶ From April to October it's compulsory to join a tour from 10am to 3pm.

▶ From April to October there's a free bus linking Auschwitz with Birkenau. It's an easy 2km walk between the two sites.

▶ Most travel agencies in Kraków offer organised tours from 130zł per person, including transport and a guide.

✗ Take a Break

There are a few snack bars near the main parking area, but for something more substantial, try the restaurant at the **Hotel Olecki** (📞 33 847 5000; www.hotelolecki. pl; ul Leszczyńskiej 12; s/d 180/210zł; P 🛜).

Washroom in the women's camp

barracks still standing and the long perimeter of barbed wire convey its enormous scale. The main building at the entrance holds a small exhibition, and you can climb the tower for a view over the camp.

Birkenau Barracks

The real experience of Birkenau is simply walking through the camp, passing through the various sections, including separate parts for men, for women, and – perversely – a small section for 'families'. You can still see the train tracks that ran through the centre of the grounds. It was here where the selection process took place: some passengers were sent to labour as slaves and live in the squalor of the barracks; others were herded off the train and sent directly to the gas chambers.

Central Baths & Gas Chambers

To the back of the Birkenau camp, you can visit the central camp baths and retrace the route of prisoners as they moved from the selection process to the gas chambers. Nearby, are the ruins of the gas chambers, crematoria, and other places where corpses were burned in the open air and the ashes deposited in small ponds.

Birkenau Main Gate & Tower

From the main camp, the tour proceeds to the largest of the outlying camps, at Birkenau, 2km to the west. Most of the mass killings actually took place at this vast expanse, which was purpose-built by the Nazis as an extermination camp. Although much of the camp was destroyed by the retreating Nazis near the end of WWII, the many

Understand

A Short Holocaust History

It goes beyond the scope of this book to describe in any detail the slaughter of Poland's Jewish population by Nazi Germany, but some background is essential to understanding the Auschwitz experience. The numbers speak for themselves: of three million Jews living in Poland in 1939, fewer than 100,000 survived WWII.

Early Stages

In the early stages of WWII, in 1940 and 1941, the Germans used camps like Auschwitz to house political prisoners, including Poles who had resisted the German invasion or posed a threat. Polish Jews were restricted to purpose-built ghettos constructed in Warsaw, Łódź, Podgórze (Kraków) and scores of other cities.

Living conditions in the ghettos were appalling and thousands died of disease and malnutrition. To this day, many Polish cities still bear the scars of their former ghettos.

From Internment to Extermination

After Germany declared war on the Soviet Union in 1941, Nazi policy toward the Jews shifted from internment to full-scale extermination. Here at Auschwitz, the Birkenau camp was built to function exclusively as a holding and extermination camp. By the end of 1942 and into early 1943, the majority of Poland's Jewry had been killed. Many victims were gassed here or at similar camps at Treblinka, Sobibór and Bełżec, while others were shot in forests around their villages.

The killings at Auschwitz-Birkenau and other places would grind on through 1944, but by then most of the victims were European Jews from outside Poland.

Supplementary Reading

A visit is certain to increase your interest in this history and there are several excellent titles available. For many, the gold standard remains Primo Levi's *Survival in Auschwitz*. Levi, an Italian Jew, survived the war as a prisoner in the Monowitz camp at Auschwitz.

To see the camps from a Polish perspective, pick up Tadeusz Borowski's *This Way for the Gas, Ladies and Gentlemen*. Borowski was not a Jew, but a Polish political prisoner.

Top Sights
Wieliczka Salt Mine

Getting There

🚌 **Bus** departs from minibus stands along ul Pawia, across from the Galeria Krakowska, to Wieliczka (3zł).

🚆 **Train** departs throughout the day from the main train station to Wieliczka (4zł, 25 minutes)

'More than salt', boasts the advert promoting a visit to this ultra-deep mine on Kraków's outskirts. But actually, it's nothing more than salt. And that's exactly why it's so impressive. It's an eerie underground world of pits and chambers, filled with finely crafted sculptures and bas-reliefs, and everything has been carved by hand from salt. The mine has been recognised as a Unesco World Heritage site for more than 30 years.

Don't Miss

Chapel of St Kinga

Tours start with a giddying descent down 380 wooden stairs to reach a depth of 135m. The showpiece is the ornamented Chapel of St Kinga (Kaplica Św Kingi), which is actually a fair-sized church measuring 54m by 18m, and 12m high. Every single element here, from chandeliers to altarpieces, is made of salt. It took over 30 years (completed in 1895) for one man and then his brother to complete this underground chapel.

Erazm Barącz Chamber

This chamber, situated at a depth of 100m, has been partly flooded by a lake. The lake is some 9m deep and the water gives off an eerie green glow because of the high saline content.

Stanisław Staszic Chamber

This enormous chamber measures 36m in height, and visitors can enjoy the scale from a lookout platform. The chamber is so large it's hosted extreme sporting events and even the world's first underground balloon flight.

Kraków Saltworks Museum

The tour ends at the Kraków Saltworks Museum, accommodated in 14 chambers on level three, but most visitors seem to be over-salted by then. From here a fast mining lift takes you back up to the real world.

☏ 12 278 7302

www.kopalnia.pl

ul Daniłowicza 10

adult/concession
79/64zł

🕑 7.30am-7.30pm Apr-Oct, 8am-5pm Nov-Mar

☑ Top Tips

▶ The guided tours take two hours and cover about 3km.

▶ Bring a coat or sweater. The temperature in the mine is a chilly 15°C.

▶ English-language tours depart every half-hour from 8.30am to 6pm in summer, and less frequently the rest of the year.

▶ Buy tickets in advance online or turn to an InfoKraków office or your hotel for help.

▶ Several tour operators, including Cracow City Tours (p142), run bus tours to the mine for 130zł per person.

✗ Take a Break

Lunch is available underground in the mine at the **The Miners' Tavern** in the Budryk Chamber.

The Best of
Kraków

Kraków's Best Walks

Kraków's Best...

St Mary's Basilica (p38)
ANDREA CASTELLANO/500PX ©

Best Walks
Christian & Jewish Kazimierz

🏃 The Walk

For centuries, Kazimierz was home to active communities of both Christians and Jews. Though divided by a wall, the two groups co-existed (largely peacefully) as they carved out separate spaces for living and worshipping. This walk takes in some of that diverse community.

Start Most Grunwaldzki 🚋 11, 18, 22, 52

Finish ul Starowiślna 🚋 3, 9, 19, 24, 50

Length 3km; two hours

🍴 Take a Break

Plac Wolnica, poised between the historic Christian and Jewish areas, is ideal for a break. **Młynek Café** (p75) is a dependable vegetarian option and good for salads or coffee. **Well Done** (p76) is a likeable burger and BBQ joint on trendy ul Mostowa.

WITOLD SKRZYPCZAK/GETTY IMAGES ©

Corpus Christi Church (p73)

❶ Pauline Church of SS Michael & Stanislaus

Pauline Church of SS Michael & Stanislaus (p73) is a mid-18th-century Baroque church that enjoys a great view over the river, but feels hidden from the city. The most interesting feature is the crypt, which holds the remains of several eminent cultural figures, including Nobel-prize-winning writer Czesław Miłosz (1911-2004).

❷ St Catherine's Church

St Catherine's (p71) dates from the very earliest days of the 14th century, when Kazimierz was a separate town from Kraków. The Gothic exterior is largely unchanged, and the spacious interior is used for concerts and festival events (in addition to mass).

❸ Corpus Christi Church

Founded in 1340, the **Corpus Christi Church** (p73) was for a time Kazimierz's parish church. The stark exterior is Gothic, but the interior is Baroque, with some early-15th-century stained-glass windows in the sanctuary.

❹ High Synagogue

Leave the historically Christian area as you walk east along ul Św Wawrzyńca to the Jewish quarter. Turn left at ul Wąska to see the evocative facade of the **High Synagogue** (p70). Today it is inactive but has a photo exhibit on the second floor.

❺ Remuh Synagogue & Cemetery

Wind your way through the narrow streets until you end up at ul Szeroka, traditionally the centre of the Jewish quarter. Although the name means 'wide street', it looks more like an elongated square. Near the northern end is the 16th-century **Remuh Synagogue** (p70) and the adjacent cemetery.

❻ Jewish Museum

Housed in the early 16th-century 'Old Synagogue' – true to its name, it's the oldest surviving synagogue in the country – this **Jewish Museum** (p70), a branch of the Historical Museum of the City of Kraków, is a great primer on local Jewish history and sacred objects.

❼ Galicia Jewish Museum

Just outside the main Jewish quarter, along gritty but gentrifying ul Dajwor, the **Galicia Jewish Museum** (p64) aims to link the city's Jewish heritage to the modern day through photographs and text.

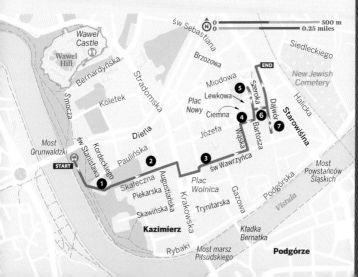

Best Walks
Route of Kings & Queens

The Walk

This walk through the Old Town follows the old coronation route for much of its way and, just as kings and queens of yesteryear aimed to do, it pays respects to the main attractions in a relatively logical path. It's a great walk for trying to hit all the key sights in the shortest amount of time.

Start Florian Gate 🚊 2, 4, 14, 19, 20, 24

Finish Wawel Hill 🚊 6, 8, 10, 13, 18

Length 2km; two hours

Take a Break

There's no shortage of places to eat or drink around Kraków's massive Rynek Główny. **Vis-à-vis** (p45), just near the Town Hall Tower, is good for beer or coffee and attracts an artistic crowd. **Arlekin** (p45), also on the Rynek, is plain but locally regarded as having the square's best cakes.

The Barbican (p49)

HENRYK T. KAISER-GETTY IMAGES ©

❶ Florian Gate

This attractive stone gateway, built in around 1300, was once the main entryway into the city and is the only one of the city's original eight gates still standing. This gate and the nearby **Barbican** bastion can be toured as part of the **City Defence Wall** (p49).

❷ St Mary's Basilica

The route continues down lively ul Floriańska. To your left as you enter the square, twin-spired **St Mary's Basilica** (p38) beckons. If you arrive near the hour, stay to hear the bugler play from the taller tower. The best place to hear the melody is in front of **St Barbara's Church**.

❸ Cloth Hall

Dominating the centre of the square is the lively **Cloth Hall** (p48), a two-level Renaissance confection that serves many purposes, including as the entryway to the **Rynek Underground** (p40). The **Gallery of 19th-Century Polish Painting** (p48) is on the second floor.

4 Town Hall Tower

The **Town Hall Tower** (p48) recalls what must have been a glorious 15th-century building before it was dismantled in the 19th century by the occupying Austrians. You can still see the original Gothic portal. Climb the tower and check out the underground space, used for concerts.

5 Collegium Maius

The **Collegium Maius** (p42) was the earliest home of Jagiellonian University, the second-oldest university in Central Europe (after Prague's Charles University). Pop in to the courtyard to see original Gothic portals and the famous clock.

6 Basilica of St Francis

Many say the **Basilica of St Francis** (p29), a 13th-century Gothic beauty, is their favourite church. Possibly it's for the dark, hushed interiors but more likely it's for the beautiful stained-glass windows. They date from the turn of the 20th century and are by Art Nouveau master Stanisław Wyspiański.

The most famous window, above the rear entrance, depicts God in the act of creation.

7 Wawel Hill

Continue south on ul Grodzka, the final stage of the Royal Route. Go as far as ul Senacka, and from there turn south onto charming ul Kanonicza. This will lead you to the foot of Wawel Hill, with **Wawel Royal Castle** (p24) and **Wawel Cathedral**.

Best
Food

By Polish standards, Kraków is a food paradise. The Old Town is packed with gastronomic venues catering for every pocket. Many are housed in vaulted cellars or quiet courtyards, offering a romantic, historic atmosphere for your meal. Aside from the wide range of Polish establishments, there is a startling number of Italian restaurants, as well as Chinese, French, Hungarian, Indian, Japanese, Mexican and more. Many restaurants in Kazimierz, particularly in the area around ul Szeroka, offer Jewish-themed cooking, complete with klezmer music.

LILECHKA75/GETTY IMAGES ©

Polish Cooking

You can't say you've eaten Polish food until you've had many plates of *pierogi*, the crescent-shaped dumplings that are stuffed with cheese, minced meat or sauerkraut. You might want to try *gołąbki* (cabbage leaves stuffed with beef and rice), but don't confuse them with *golonka* (boiled pig's knuckle). If there is one dish that is more Polish than any other, it's *bigos* (pictured above). Sauerkraut, fresh cabbage, mushrooms and meat (usually pork, game, sausage and/or bacon) cooked together over a low flame – the longer the better.

Dining on a Budget

There is no shortage of fine-dining establishments, but budget travellers will also be delighted by their options. Kraków has plenty of low-cost eateries called *bar mleczny* (milk bars) or *jadłodajnia* (like 'diner'). They offer affordable and filling Polish food, often served cafeteria-style so you know exactly what you're getting. Other options include the many vegetarian and vegan food bars around town.

☑ Top Tips

▶ Expect slow service. To speed things up, grab your own menu when you enter a restaurant; they will likely be stacked by the door.

▶ In milk bars and self-service restaurants you're often expected to clear your own table. Take your dirty plates and cutlery to a window that leads to the kitchen for cleaning.

▶ Servers will expect a tip of around 10%. Leave the gratuity in the pouch that the bill is brought in or hand the money directly to the wait-person.

KAMIL MACNIAK/GETTY IMAGES ©

Traditional Polish *pierogi* (dumplings)

Best Polish Food

Marchewka z Groszkiem Traditional Polish cooking with sidewalk tables perched on one of Kazimierz's most-happening streets. (p74)

U Babci Maliny Hearty Polish staples served in a partially hidden location, accessed through a courtyard. (p54)

Sąsiedzi Michelin-recommended Polish classics in a garden setting. (p74)

Best for Fine Dining

Cyrano de Bergerac Excellent French cooking served in an Old Town Gothic cellar. (p53)

Trufla Exquisite Italian fare at affordable prices, and a lovely Tuscan garden out back. (p52)

ZaKładka Food & Wine Upscale bistro fare in an up-and-coming part of Podgórze. (p90)

Best Vegetarian

Glonojad Popular lunch spot features meatless curries, burritos, pastas and soups. (p108)

Momo Nice range of hot and cold vegetarian mains, plus gluten-free cakes and fruit crumbles. (p75)

Restauracja Pod Norenami Meatless Asian-fusion with lots of spicy noodle and rice dishes (p101)

Best Milk Bars

Polskie Smaki Affordable spread of stuffed peppers, pork cutlets and fried livers served under a Gothic vaulted ceiling. (p54)

Bar Grodzki All the usual milk-bar treats, like *pierogi* and pork cutlets, with the added – unexpected – treat of friendly service. (p32)

Milkbar Tomasza Modern, hipsterish take on a classic milk bar, with an updated menu of curries and toasted sandwiches. (p54)

Best
Drinking & Nightlife

Kraków has an endless array of drinking establishments. Some are basement bars, while others are courtyard cafes. Some have quirky themes, while others are a hotchpotch. Some have art exhibits, while others have reading materials and board games. Some go for old-world charm, while others exude contemporary hip. There's something for everybody, really.

Bar or Cafe?

In Kraków, it's not often easy to tell the difference. The Kraków drinking scene is dominated by two types of venues: creative cafes that also serve alcohol, and bohemian bars that also serve coffee. In both, you can also normally grab a bite to eat. Indeed, whatever the primary purpose, Kraków specialises in places with an artsy atmosphere, usually furnished with mismatched chairs and tables, eclectic artwork, and casually cool-looking patrons. Not too posh, but not too pleb either, these places welcome all (but not overenthusiastically).

Clubbing

With tens of thousands of university students, it's a safe assumption that nightlife – particularly from Thursday to Sunday – revolves around clubbing. The scene, truth be told, is not much different from any other similarly sized European city, but the venues – often in Old Town cellars – lend a local flavour. The places listed below normally feature DJs or recorded music. For live bands, check under the Best Music heading (p132).

HENRYK T. KAISER/GETTY IMAGES ©

☑ Top Tips

▶ There are several brands of good, locally brewed Polish *piwo* (beer), such as Żywiec, Tyskie, Okocim and Lech, as well as a growing number of microbreweries. This blog has a great roundup of Polish breweries big and small: www.beerguide.pl.

Popular Polish brand of beer, Żywiec

Best Cafes

Café Bunkier Arty cafe and popular lunch spot, perched right on the Planty. (p56)

Café Camelot Kraków in a nutshell: cosy, candle-lit and still very cool. (p56)

Coffee Cargo Third-wave coffee roaster in a rehabbed former warehouse space, in up-and-coming Podgórze. (p91)

Cheder Strong coffee brewed in a traditional Turkish copper pot, dotted with cinnamon and cardamom. (p78)

Arlekin There are fancier places on the Rynek for coffee and cake, but this is the place that locals choose. (p45)

Mleczarnia Dark, intimate cafe is the perfect spot for a tête-à-tête over coffees or drinks. (p78)

Best Pubs & Bars

Ambasada Śledzia Cheap vodka shots served with a side of pickled herring. Need we say more? (p56)

Black Gallery Anything goes...either in the bar downstairs or the lush garden out back. (p57)

Miejsce Bar Trendy retro '50s decor, gay-friendly and great cocktails. (p78)

Singer Café Forget the 'cafe' part of the name: one of the original Kazimierz haunts comes alive after dark. (p78)

Best Clubs

Re Old-school basement club with the added attraction of a popular beer garden for those in the know. (p59)

Prozak 2.0 Big, brash dance club with a taste for electronica (p34)

Hush Live One of the few clubs in Poland to specialise in a type of cheeseball (in a good way) dance music known locally as 'Disco Polo' (p57)

Cocon Music Club One of Kraków's few surviving gay nightclubs draws big crowds on the weekend. (p79)

Best
Historic Sites

The history of Poland's former royal capital reads like an epic novel, filled with plenty of periods when it seems all is lost, only to have greatness restored at the very last moment.

IMAGE BY TOMASZ KALARUS/THE HISTORICAL MUSEUM OF THE CITY OF CRACOW ©

Royal Capital

Kraków became the capital of Poland in 1038 and was centred near Wawel Castle. The capital was burned to the ground in 1241 by marauding Tatars, but enterprising residents took the opportunity to move the city to its current location around the market square and to surround it with impenetrable walls. Under the enlightened leadership of Kazimierz III Wielki (Casimir III the Great; 1333–70), the city thrived. Its success is symbolised by the founding of Jagiellonian University in 1364.

Demotion & Decline

The city's status slipped badly in 1596 when Poland's capital was moved to a rival city, Warsaw, though Kraków remained the site of coronations and royal burials. The move prompted several centuries of decline, culminating in a decision by the occupying Austrian Empire to relegate the city to the peripheral province of Galicia in the 19th century.

World War & Communism

After independent Poland was restored following WWI, Kraków once again thrived – but another bout of tragedy was just around the corner with WWII. The German occupation during the war led to the murder of the city's academic elite and the slaughter of tens of thousands of its Jewish citizens in the Holocaust. The communist government added more misery by building a heavily polluting steelworks at Nowa Huta.

Best Royal History

Wawel Royal Castle The centre of power for five centuries and the enduring emblem of the Polish state. (p24)

Collegium Maius The oldest surviving university building in Poland, and one of the best examples of Gothic architecture in the city. (p42)

Cloth Hall The focal point of the grand Rynek Główny and once the centre of Kraków's medieval cloth trade. (p48)

Wawel Royal Castle (p24)

MENZHAIN/GETTY IMAGES ©

Best Churches

St Mary's Basilica The church's two uneven towers are the symbol of the city. (p38)

Wawel Cathedral Witness to countless coronations and the final resting place of Polish monarchs, heroes and presidents. (p26)

Basilica of St Francis Gorgeous church enlivened by fantastic Art Nouveau stained-glass windows by artist Stanisław Wyspiański. (p29)

Best Museums

Rynek Underground The 'Middle Ages meets 21st century' experience is enhanced by holograms and audiovisual wizardry. (pictured top left; p40)

Museum of Pharmacy One of the largest museums of its kind anywhere, with heaps of old lab equipment and rare pharmaceutical instruments. (p48)

Historical Museum of Kraków Home to an engaging, interactive exhibition that charts the city from its earliest days to WWI. (p49)

Worth A Trip

Twelve kilometres southwest of the centre, the **Benedictine Abbey of SS Peter & Paul** (Opactwo Benedyktynów w Tyńcu; ☎12 688 5450; www.tyniec.benedyktyni.pl; ul Benedyktyńska 37, Tyniec; museum adult/concession 7/5zł, church free; ⏱museum 10am-6pm; ☒112) dramatically rises on a cliff above the Vistula. To reach the abbey, take bus 112 from the Rondo Grunwaldzkie, the roundabout on the west side of Grunwald Bridge.

Best
Music

Southern Poland's leading cultural centre is no slouch when it comes to the performing arts, classical music and opera. Kraków also has a long tradition in jazz and some of the country's most historic jazz clubs. Thousands of students ensure a lively club and indie scene, with many of the best shows in rehabbed factories and industrial sites.

Best Live Music

Alchemia Kazimierz's best drinking spot holds live gigs in the basement through the week. (pictured above; p78)

Fabryka Klub Former factory in Podgórze has become the city's leading venue for indie and experimental live music. (p93)

Piwnica Pod Baranami Awesome pub, transformed some nights into cabaret, jazz bar or jam session. (p45)

Best for Jazz

Harris Piano Jazz Bar Serious jazz in an atmospheric cellar space below the main square. (p58)

Piec' Art Intimate basement bar and jazz club that's a seductive place for a drink even when it's quiet. (p59)

Jazz Club U Muniaka Well-known jazz outlet just a couple steps from the market square. (p59)

Best Classical & Opera

Opera Krakowska The Kraków Opera performs in the striking, modern building, but the repertoire spans the ages. (p110)

Filharmonia Krakowska Home to one of the best orchestras in the country. (p103)

☑ **Top Tips**

▸ The InfoKraków (p150) tourist office in the Old Town specialises in tickets and cultural events.

▸ Many festivals are built around a music theme. Check out www.krakowfestival. com for a list of festivals in English.

Bonerowski Palace Regular evening piano recitals of music by Fryderyk Chopin, Poland's best-known composer. (p59)

KAY MAERITZ/LOOK-FOTO/GETTY IMAGES ©

Best
Art

As the former capital of a strongly Catholic country, Kraków has an amazing collection of religious art in churches and museums going back centuries. It was also the centre of the *Młoda Polska* (Young Poland) movement in visual arts at the start of the 20th century that left the city with an impressive heritage of Art Nouveau works.

LONELY PLANET/GETTY IMAGES ©

Best Museums

National Museum The Gallery of 20th-Century Polish Painting is a treasure chest of early-modern weirdness from the likes of Stanisław Wyspiański and Witkacy. (p98)

Archdiocesan Museum A vast collection of religious sculpture and paintings, dating from the 13th to 16th centuries and located in a 14th-century townhouse. (p29)

Gallery of 19th-Century Polish Painting The Chełmoński room, one of four separate collections here, holds important works in the Realist, Impressionist and Symbolist schools. (p48)

Museum of Contemporary Art in Kraków Cutting-edge modern painting and visual arts, in an industrial setting just beside Schindler's Factory. (p89)

Best Galleries

Raven Gallery Private gallery, lovingly curated, with beautiful examples of Cubist and Socialist-Realist paintings. (p67)

Starmach Gallery Exhibits contemporary Polish painting and sculpture from a gallery housed in a former Jewish prayer house. (p93)

Jan Fejkiel Gallery Specialises in contemporary prints and drawings, with a focus on emerging artists. (p61)

Galeria Dyląg We love this private art gallery of modern works from the 1940s to the 1970s, including Polish drip

☑ **Top Tip**

▶ Check out the offerings on the website of the **Szołayski House** (☎ 12 433 5450; www.muzeum.krakow.pl; ul Szczepańska 9; adult/concession 11/7zł, free Sun; ⏰ 10am-6pm Tue-Sat, 10am-4pm Sun; 🚊 2, 4, 8, 13, 14, 18, 20, 24), a former museum that now houses rotating exhibitions.

paintings reminiscent of Jackson Pollock. (p59)

Galeria Plakatu Beautifully crafted film posters stuffed into every nook and cranny of this evocative Old Town shop. (pictured above; p60)

Best
Architecture

Poland's architecture styles have followed Western Europe over the centuries. The earliest style, Romanesque, dates from the 12th and 13th centuries but little has survived. There are ample remnants, however, of Gothic, Baroque and more modern styles like Art Nouveau.

High Gothic

Gothic architecture, with its elongated, pointed arches and ribbed vaults, began in the 14th century and lasted around 200 years. It's associated with the prosperous reign of King Kazimierz III Wielki and is seen in important churches such as Wawel Cathedral and St Mary's Basilica.

Baroque & Neoclassical

Baroque, strongly associated with the Catholic Church and the Counter-Reformation, swept aside almost all other styles by the 17th century. Lavish and highly decorative, it altered existing architecture by adding its sumptuous decor to interiors, particularly churches, around the city.

Art Nouveau & Socialist-Realist

The sinuous lines and plant motifs of the Art Nouveau style are evident in buildings embellished by local artists such as Józef Mehoffer and Stanisław Wyspiański. The lows came a few decades later in the grimmer communist period, though the Nowa Huta district east of the centre shows off an arguably more positive side of Socialist-Realist architecture.

TOMASZ MAZON/SHUTTERSTOCK ©

☑ **Top Tip**

▶ To see one of the only surviving remnants of Romanesque architecture in Kraków, check out the facade of the Church of St Andrew (p31).

Best Gothic

St Catherine's Church
Enormous 14th-century church has retained its original Gothic proportions over the years. (p71)

City Defence Walls The Florian Gate was once the city's main entrance and dates from the 14th century. (p49)

Holy Trinity Basilica
The Dominican Church is defined by its gorgeous

BRENIK/SHUTTERSTOCK ©

Church of St Anne (p50)

14th-century Gothic portal. (pictured above left; p50)

Best Baroque

Church of SS Peter & Paul Eye-catching statues line the exterior of the city's first Baroque building. (p31)

Church of St Anne Considered one of the country's best examples of classical Baroque design. (p50)

Best Art Nouveau

Noworolski Peek inside this Rynek cafe to admire the stunning Art Nouveau interiors by Polish artist Józef Mehoffer. (p45)

Palace of Fine Arts The most impressive edifice

on Art Nouveau–friendly Plac Szczepański. (p50)

Narodowy Stary Teatr The lavish Art Nouveau exterior was designed by sculptor Józef Gardecki in 1906. (p59)

Best Communist

Forum Przestrzenie The brutalist Hotel Forum has been given a retro makeover and is now one of the city's coolest bars. (p92)

Arka Pana Eyesore or eye-catching, this modern church was the first place of worship to be built in Nowa Huta. (p113)

Teatr Ludowy Excellent example of Socialist-Realist architecture from the 1950s. (p113)

Worth a Trip

The small, wooden **Church of St Bartholomew** (Kościół Św Bartłomieja; 📞 12 644 2331; www. mogila.cystersi.pl; ul Klasztorna 11; 🕐 10am-6pm Thu-Sat, noon-5pm Sun; 🚌 10, 16) in Nowa Huta defies architectural classification. It dates from the mid-15th century, which makes it Poland's oldest surviving three-nave timber church. As an aside, it was one of only two churches available to workers in Nowa Huta, until the Arka Pana church was built in 1977.

Best
Shopping

Although Kraków is not exactly a shopping destination, it's easy to while away an afternoon snooping in souvenir shops, browsing bookstores and inspecting art galleries. The Old Town is packed with shops selling tacky T-shirts, gorgeous glassware and everything in between. There is also a variety of high-end art galleries and antique shops.

KRZYSZTOF DYDYNSKI/GETTY IMAGES ©

Polish Souvenirs

If you're in the market for the perfect Polish souvenir, you'll have plenty of options. You can't go wrong with typical Polish food and drink. One staple is locally made vodka, but Poland also makes very good chocolates, honeys and jams. Poland is also known for its glassware and ceramics, particularly the colourful plates, jugs and vases from the western Polish town of Bolesławiec. There's a wide selection of handmade jewellery, including exquisite original pieces.

Amber, Amber & (More) Amber

Amber – otherwise known as 'Baltic gold' – is a piece of fossilised tree resin, usually found on the shores of the Baltic Sea. When it's cut and buffed it makes for a beautiful semi-precious stone in a ring, necklace or brooch. If you're not planning a trip to Gdańsk or another northern Polish city, then by all means Kraków has plenty of galleries with beautiful and original designs and settings. Make sure to look around as prices can vary considerably.

Best Food & Drink

Produkty Benedyktyńskie
Cheeses, wines, cookies and honey, all made by Benedictine monks. (p80)

Krakowska Manufaktura Czekolady Gorgeous homemade chocolates already wrapped up as gifts, with a little cafe upstairs where you can enjoy a hot chocolate beverage. (p61)

Best Glassware & Cermics

Kobalt Eye-poppingly beautiful ceramic designs from the western Polish city of Bolesławiec. (p35)

Cloth Hall (p48)

CAHA Art Original, hand-painted ceramic plates, cups, dishes and dolls given a colourful, playful twist. (p66)

Marka High-concept design store that sells a range of items, including dishes, cups and glasses in amusing retro shapes and colours. (p67)

Best Jewellery

Błażko Jewellery Design Chequered enamel rings, pendants and bracelets from the workshop of local legend Grzegorz Błażko. (p67)

My Gallery Dramatic designs inspired by nature. (p61)

Danutta Hand Gallery Collective of local artisans with an eye for turning spare parts and found objects into stylish accessories like cuff links and earrings. (p67)

Best for Amber

Boruni Amber Museum Cases of amber jewellery plus a small 'museum' where you can learn how amber is cut and set. (p61)

Boruni Gallery Beautiful showroom, featuring a range of colours in high-end settings. (p35)

Amber Slightly more downmarket, with a nice selection of amber pieces but at affordable prices. (p35)

Best Markets

Cloth Hall For a great selection of classic Polish souvenirs, look no further than this giant building on the Rynek Główny. (p48)

Hala Targowa Old books, maps, a bit of junk and heaps of cheap clothing. (p111)

Plac Nowy Kazimierz flea market best on Saturday and Sunday mornings. (p80)

Stary Kleparz For food and picnic provisions, check out the stalls here. (p103)

Best
Jewish Heritage

Kraków, more particularly Kazimierz, was an important centre of Jewish life and culture for centuries. This cultural vibrancy vanished overnight, due to the mass deportation and extermination of the Jewish people at the hands of the German Nazis during WWII. This deep legacy has left the city with arguably Central Europe's most important collection of Jewish heritage sights.

MARIUSZ S JURGIELEWICZ/SHUTTERSTOCK ©

Best Museums

Galicia Jewish Museum
This museum both commemorates Jewish victims of the Holocaust and celebrates the Jewish culture and history of the former Austro-Hungarian region of Galicia. (p64)

Jewish Museum
Housed in the Old Synagogue, which dates from the 15th century, with exhibitions on liturgical objects and lots of moving photographs. (p70)

Schindler's Factory
Impressive interactive museum covers the Nazi occupation of Kraków in WWII, housed in the former enamel factory of Oskar Schindler. (p84)

Best Synagogues

High Synagogue
This place of worship was built around 1560, and is the third-oldest synagogue in Kraków after the Old and Remuh Synagogues. (p70)

Remuh Synagogue
The area's smallest synagogue and one of only two regularly used for religious services. (p70)

Isaac Synagogue
Kraków's largest synagogue has been restored and now houses a permanent exhibition titled 'In Memory of Polish Jews'. (p70)

Best Other Sights

Remuh Cemetery
Tiny burial ground situated just off of ul Szeroka in

☑ Top Tips

▸ Try the Austeria (p81) bookshop in Kazimierz for an excellent selection of Jewish and Holocaust literature in English, plus posters and music CDs.

▸ The Jarden Tourist Agency (p70) in Kazimierz offers several Jewish-themed walking and bus tours.

Kazimierz. The cemetery was spared being damaged by the Nazis during WWII. (p71)

New Jewish Cemetery
Highly moving burial ground that survived the Holocaust. Some 9000 tombstones are visible. (p108)

Best
With Kids

Poles are very family-oriented, and there are plenty of activities for children around the city. An increasing number of restaurants cater specifically to children, with play areas and so on, and many offer a children's menu; even if they don't, they can usually provide smaller portions for a lower price. Kids normally pay half price for attractions up to age 15 (under five free) and it's the same on public transport. Kids aged between five and 15 years old pay half price.

KRZYSZTOF DYDYNSKI/GETTY IMAGES ©

Hiflyer Balon Widokowy
For fabulous views of Wawel Royal Castle and the Old Town, it's hard to beat the Hiflyer hot-air balloon. (p100)

Horse-Drawn Carriages
It'll cost you a pretty penny, but what small child could resist a ride in a real horse-drawn carriage? The carriages line up at the northern end of Rynek Główny. (p51)

Ster River cruises around the city or as far as Tyniec Abbey aboard the *Sobieski*, berthed not far from the Dębnicki Bridge, below the Sheraton Kraków hotel and accessed from ul Zwierzyniecka. (p100)

Zoological Gardens
These 20-hectare zoological gardens are home to thousands of animals. Bus 134 heads to the zoo from its terminus near

the National Museum. (p99)

Wieliczka Salt Mine
Kids, particularly young teens, will be impressed by the deep descent into Poland's most famous salt mine. (p118)

Dragon's Den The sights of the Wawel Castle, while fascinating for adults, will likely be soporific for kids after an hour or two. The cheesy dragon's den, however, complete with fire-breathing dragon, will delight small children. (p26)

Worth A Trip

Your skin will be wrinkled and prunelike by the time you leave this fun-filled **Park Wodny** (☎12 616 3190; www.parkwodny.pl; ul Dobrego Pasterza 126; per hr adult/concession Mon-Fri 23/19zł, Sat & Sun 25/22zł, all day incl sauna weekdays 52/40zł, weekend 58/45zł; ⏱8am-10pm; ☐129, 152), an aqua park located 2.5km northeast of the Old Town. For endless hours of wet and wild, there are paddling pools, water sports, 800m of water slides, saltwater hot tubs, saunas and more.

Best
Festivals & Events

Kraków has one of the richest cycles of annual events in Poland. Indeed, the summer months are crammed with overlapping festivals to the point where even locals say there might be too much of a good thing. The first port of call for information is the nearest branch of the InfoKraków tourist office.

DE VISU/SHUTTERSTOCK ©

Winter (January–March)

New Year's Concert (☻Jan) Kraków ushers in the New Year with classical music at the Teatr im Słowackiego, while plebs make do with fireworks and rock bands in the Rynek.

Shanties International Festival of Sailors' Songs (www.shanties.pl; ☻Feb) Going strong since 1981, despite Kraków's inland location.

Bach Days (www.bach-cantatas.com; ☻Mar) Baroque fugues presented at the Academy of Music.

Spring (April–June)

Cracovia Marathon (www.zis.krakow.pl; ☻Apr) Increasingly popular international running event.

International Soup Festival (Międzynarodowy Festiwal Zupy; www.teatrkto.pl; ☻May) A day in May dedicated to cooking and eating soup on Plac Nowy.

Juvenalia (www.juwenalia.krakow.pl; ☻May) During this student carnival, students receive symbolic keys to the town's gates and take over the city for four days and three nights.

Krakow Film Festival (www.kff.com.pl; ☻May-Jun) Film festival that's been going for more than half a century screens hundreds of movies from various countries.

☑ **Top Tip**

▶ The **Kraków Festival Guide** website (www.krakowfestival.com) maintains a handy list of festivals in English.

Lajkonik Pageant (www.mhk.pl; ☻May-Jun) Takes place seven days after Corpus Christi. This colourful pageant is headed by the Lajkonik, a comical figure disguised as a bearded Tatar.

Rękawka (Podgórze; www.podgorze.pl; near the Church of St Benedict; ☻Apr-May) A spring festival dating to pagan times. Festivities take place near the Church of St Benedict on the Tuesday after Easter.

Participants at the spring festival Rękawka

Summer (July-September)

Jewish Culture Festival

(www.jewishfestival.pl) Features a variety of cultural events including theatre, film, music and art exhibitions, and concludes with a grand open-air klezmer concert on ul Szeroka.

International Summer Organ Concert

(www.dworek.krakow.pl; ⏱ Jul-Aug) Organ recitals scheduled in several city churches.

International Festival of Street Theatre

(www.teatrkto.pl; ⏱ Jul) Takes place on the main market square.

Rozstaje

(Crossroads; ☎ 603 944 988; www.etnokrakow.pl; ⏱ July) Sometimes referred to as 'EtnoKraków' – a week-long celebration of world and ethnic music featuring musicians from countries around the world.

Festival of Music in Old Cracow

(www.capellacracoviensis.pl; ⏱ Jul-Aug) Important musical event that goes on for two weeks and spans five centuries of musical tradition from medieval to contemporary.

Pierogi Festival

(www.biurofestiwalowe.pl; ⏱ Aug) Three-day celebration of the mighty dumpling, held in the Mały Rynek (Small Market Sq) east of St Mary's Basilica.

Summer Jazz Festival

(www.cracjazz.com; ⏱ Jul-Aug) Featuring the best of Polish modern jazz.

Sacrum Profanum

(www.biurofestiwalowe.pl; ⏱ Sep) Classical music festival dedicated to the composers of a different country each year.

Autumn (October-December)

Zaduszki Jazz Festival

(⏱ Oct-Nov) Jazz staged at venues around the city.

Kraków Christmas Crib Competition

(www.szopki.eu; ⏱ Dec) Competition held on the first Thursday of December to see who can build the best 'crib', which is something like an especially elaborate nativity scene.

Best
Tours

ANTON_IVANOV/SHUTTERSTOCK ©

Best Bus & Golf Cart Tours

Cracow Sightseeing Tours
(☎795 003 231; www.cracow-redbus.com; 48-hr ticket adult/concession 90/70zł) Decent range of city walking and bus tours, including a popular four-hour bus tour, as well as longer day excursions to the Wieliczka Salt Mine and Auschwitz-Birkenau Memorial & Museum.

Cracow City Tours
(☎12 421 2864; www.cracowcity-tours.pl; ul Floriańska 44; city tour adult/concession 120/100zł; ☉9.30am-9.30pm May-Sep, 10am-8pm Oct-Apr; ☐2, 4, 14, 19, 20, 24) 'Jump-on, jump-off' double-decker bus, with departure points around the city. Consult the website for map and timetable.

Krak Tour
(☎886 664 999; www.kraktour.pl) No bus can get you around the narrow streets of the Old Town and Kazimierz like these five-seater golf carts.

Best Walking (& Crawling) Tours

Free Walking Tour
(Map p46, C5; ☎513 875 815; www.freewalkingtour.com; ☐1, 6, 8, 13, 18) Free tour of the Old Town and Kazimierz provided by licensed tour guides who make their money from tips. Tours depart daily from near the Rynek Główny.

Krakow Pub Crawl
(Map p46, C5; www.krawl-throughkrakow.com; Rynek Główny; 60zł; ☉9pm May-Oct; ☐1, 6, 8, 13, 18) Visit four venues, with unlimited drinks for an hour at the first bar. Meets nightly (9pm May-Oct) on the Rynek Główny (in front of the Adam Mickiewicz Statue).

Best Special Interest Tours

Crazy Guides
(☎500 091 200; www.crazyguides.com) Highly entertaining tours of the communist-era suburbs, including a 2½-hour tour to Nowa Huta (139zł) in an East German Trabant car.

Jarden Tourist Agency
(☎12 421 7166; www.jarden.pl; ul Szeroka 2; ☐3, 9, 19, 24, 50) Jewish-themed tours, including two- and three-hour walking tours of Kazimierz and Podgórze, as well as a two-hour tour of places made famous by *Schindler's List*.

Survival Guide

Survival Guide

Before You Go

When To Go

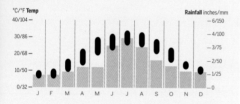

➡ **Winter** (Nov–Mar)
Short, dark days, snow
and blustery winds. Tour-
ists descend for lively
Christmas and New Year
festivities.

➡ **Spring** (Apr–Jun) April
marks the start of the
tourist season. Accom-
modation tightens over
Easter.

➡ **Summer** (Jul–Aug)
Sunny and occasionally
hot. Tourist levels on the
Rynek swell to bursting.

➡ **Autumn** (Sep–Oct)
Occasionally sunny but
cool. Some attractions
close for winter.

Book Your Stay
☑ **Top Tip** Book in ad-
vance to ensure your top
choice in accommodation
and take advantage of
cheaper rates.

➡ Air-conditioning isn't
necessary most of the
year; the exception is July
and August, when Kraków
is prone to an occasional
heat wave.

➡ Parking can be tight. If
driving, work out parking
details with the hotel in
advance.

➡ To save money, con-
sider booking a private
single or double in a
hostel.

➡ If noise is an issue, ask
for a room away from the
street. Bear in mind top-
floor rooms, immediately
below the roof, can be hot
in summer.

Useful Websites

Booking (www.booking.com) Biggest aggregator of hotels in Poland.

Hamilton Suites (www.krakow-apartments.biz) Specialises in short-term apartment rental.

Lonely Planet (www.lonelyplanet.com/krakow) Traveller forum and listings.

Airbnb (www.airbnb.com) Big section on Kraków for peer-to-peer apartment and room rentals.

Best Budget

Mundo Hostel (www.mundohostel.eu) Attractive, well-maintained hostel in a quiet courtyard location, neatly placed between the Old Town and Kazimierz.

Greg & Tom Hostel (www.gregtomhostel.com) Well-run hostel spread over three locations. Staff are friendly, the rooms are clean and laundry facilities are included.

Good Bye Lenin Hostel (www.goodbyelenin.pl) Cheerful place has a cheeky communist theme with absurd paintings and statues mocking the imagery of the era.

Hostel Flamingo (www.flamingo-hostel.com) Highly rated hostel with an excellent central location, just a couple of steps from the main square.

Best Midrange

Wielopole (www.wielopole.pl) Bright, modern rooms – all of them with spotless bathrooms – is housed in a renovated block with a great courtyard on the eastern edge of the Old Town.

Hotel Eden (www.hoteleden.pl) Located within three meticulously restored 15th-century townhouses, complete with a sauna and the only mikvah (traditional Jewish bath) in Kraków.

Hotel Pod Wawelem (www.hotelpodwawelem.pl) This hotel, overlooking the river, gets high marks for crisp, up-to-date design and an excellent breakfast buffet.

U Pana Cogito (www.pcogito.pl) White and cream seem to be the colours of choice at this friendly 14-room hotel, in a lovely mansion across the river from the centre.

Best Top End

Hotel Pod Różą (www.podroza.hotel) Antiques, oriental carpets, a wonderful glassed-in courtyard restaurant and state-of-the-art facilities.

Hotel Stary (www.stary.hotel.com.pl) Setting a high standard, the Stary is housed in an 18th-century aristocratic residence that exudes charm.

Metropolitan Boutique Hotel (www.hotelmetropolitan.pl) This luxury boutique fuses modern design within the confines of a 19th-century townhouse.

Hotel Pugetów (www.donimirski.com) Charming boutique hotel standing proudly next to the 19th-century neo-Renaissance palace. Think embroidered bathrobes, black-marble baths and a fabulous breakfast room in the basement.

Arriving in Kraków

☑ **Top Tip** For the best way to get to your accommodation, see p17

John Paul II International Airport

Kraków's main international gateway, **John Paul II International Airport** (KRK; ☎information 12 295 5800; www.krakowairport.pl; Kapitana Mieczysława Medweckiego 1, Balice; 🛜), is in Balice, 11km west of the city. Facilities include a bar and restaurant, information desks, car-rental agencies, accommodation agencies, bank ATMs and money-exchange offices.

➡ **Trains** depart once or twice an hour between 4am and 11.30pm, running to Kraków Główny train station. To reach the train, take a free shuttle bus to a nearby train station. Buy tickets on board (10zł) for the 18-minute journey.

➡ **Public buses** 292 and 208 run from the airport to Kraków's main bus station and require a 4zł ticket.

➡ A **taxi** between the airport and the city centre costs about 90zł.

Kraków Główny Train Station

Remodelled and gleaming **Kraków Główny Train Station** (Map p106, B3; Dworzec Główny; ☎information 22 391 9757; www.pkp.pl; Plac Dworcowy; 🚊2, 3, 4, 10, 14, 19, 24, 52), on the northern outskirts of the Old Town, handles international trains and most domestic rail services. Enter and exit the station through the Galeria Krakowska shopping centre.

➡ **Walk** to the Old Town in about 10 minutes by following ul Pawia south.

➡ **Trams** connect the station to all parts of the city. Most trams stop south of the station, on the northern edge of the Old Town.

Kraków Bus Station

Nearly all international and domestic coaches use Kraków's modern **bus station** (Map p106, B3; ☎703 403 340; www.mda. malopolska.pl; ul Bosacka 18; ⊙information 7am-8pm; 🚊2, 3, 4, 10, 14, 19, 24, 52).

The station is adjacent to the Kraków Główny Train Station on the northern fringe of the Old Town. Enter and exit the station through the Galeria Krakowska shopping centre.

➡ **Walk** to the Old Town in about 10 minutes by following ul Pawia south.

➡ **Trams** connect the station to all parts of the city. Most trams stop south of the station, on the northern edge of the Old Town.

Getting Around

Most tourist attractions in the centre are within easy walking distance. For longer distances, Kraków has a cheap and efficient **public transport system** (Miejskie Przedsiębiorstwo Komunikacyjne/MPK; ☎19150; www.mpk.krakow. pl) of trams and buses.

Trams & Buses

☑ **Best for...** Moving from the centre of the city to outlying areas or going from the Old Town to Podgórze.

➡ Trams and buses run between 5am and 11pm.

➡ Several types of tickets and passes are available.

➡ Buy tickets from machines located on board vehicles (have coins ready) or from news kiosks at important stops.

➡ Remember to validate your ticket in stamping machines when you board; spot checks are frequent.

Taxis

☑ **Best for**... Late-night rides back to the hotel, airport transfers and when you're running late.

➡ While the number of rogue drivers has decreased in recent years, it's better to order a taxi by phone rather than hail one off the street.

➡ The meter starts at 7zł and rises 2.30zł per kilometre travelled. Rates rise to 3.50zł per kilometre from 10pm to 6am and on Sundays.

➡ Companies that employ reliable drivers and can handle requests in English include **iTaxi** (☎737 737 737; www.itaxi.pl), **Euro Taxi** (☎12 266 6111, 12 19664) and **Lajkonik Taxi** (☎12 19628).

Bicycle

☑ **Best for**... Sightseeing and riding along the river.

➡ Despite heavy traffic, ubiquitous golf carts ferrying tourists, horse carriages and trams, Kraków has become more bike-friendly.

➡ For rentals, recommended outfitters (closed winter) include **Dwa Koła** (☎12 421 5785; ul Józefa 5; per 3hr/day 20/40zł; ⏱10am-6pm; 🚊6, 8, 10, 13) and **Krk Bike Rental** (☎509 267 733; www.krkbikerental.pl; ul Św Anny 4; per hour/day 9/50zł; 🚊2, 13, 18, 20).

Essential Information

Business Hours

Most places adhere to the hours below. Shopping centres have longer hours and are open daily from 9am to 8pm. Museums are usually closed on Mondays.

Banks 8am to 5pm Monday to Friday

Offices 8am to 5pm Monday to Friday

Shops 9am to 6pm Monday to Friday, 10am to 2pm or 3pm Saturday

Tickets & Passes

Tickets are interchangeable on trams and buses. Buy tickets at newsstands near tram stops or at automated ticket machines on board. If you're staying longer than a few hours, buy a day or multiday pass. Options include:

Basic ticket Valid 40 minutes; adult/concession 3.80/1.90zł

Short-term ticket Valid 20 minutes; adult/concession 2.80/1.40zł

One-day ticket Valid 24 hours; adult/concession 15/7.50zł

Two-day ticket Valid 48 hours; adult/concession 24/12zł

Three-day ticket Valid 72 hours; adult/concession 36/18zł

Restaurants Breakfast from 9am or 10am to noon, lunch noon to 3pm, dinner from 6pm to 11pm daily

Discount Cards

The **Krakow Card** (www.krakowcard.com) available from InfoKraków tourist information offices, includes travel on public transport and entry to many museums (2/3 days 100/120zł). It's worth the investment if you plan on seeing several museums.

Electricity

230V/50Hz

Emergency

General emergency
☑112 (mobile phone only)

Ambulance ☑999

Fire ☑998

Police ☑997

Money

The official Polish currency is the złoty, abbreviated to zł. It's divided into 100 groszy, abbreviated to gr. Banknotes come in denominations of 10zł, 20zł, 50zł, 100zł and 200zł, and coins in 1gr, 2gr, 5gr, 10gr, 20gr and 50gr, and 1zł, 2zł and 5zł. Hold on to coins and small notes for tram tickets and cafes.

ATMs

➡ ATMs are ubiquitous, particularly along main streets or in neighbourhood centres.

➡ ATMs accept both Visa and MasterCard, as well as other international cash cards. ATMs require a four-digit PIN code.

➡ Instead of exchanging cash, withdraw cash as needed from an ATM. Conversion fees are normally better than banks or exchange counters.

Cash

➡ Change money at banks or *kantors* (private currency-exchange offices). Find these along main streets as well as at travel agencies, train stations and post offices. Rates vary, so it's best to shop around.

➡ *Kantors* are usually open between 9am and 6pm on weekdays and to 2pm on Saturday, but some open longer and a few stay open 24 hours.

➡ *Kantors* exchange cash only. The most common and easily changed are US dollars, euros and UK pounds.

Credit Cards

➡ Major credit cards, like Visa and MasterCard, are widely accepted for goods and services. You may experience a problem with small transactions (under 10zł).

➡ American Express cards are typically accepted at larger hotels and restaurants, though they are not as widely recognised as other cards.

Tipping

➡ In restaurants, tip 10% to reward good service. Leave the tip in the pouch the bill is delivered in or hand the money directly to the server.

➡ Tip hairdressers, tour guides and other personal services 10% of the total.

➡ Taxis drivers won't expect a tip, but it's fine to round the fare up to the nearest 10zł increment.

Public Holidays

New Year's Day 1 January

Epiphany 6 January

Easter Sunday March or April

Easter Monday March or April

State Holiday 1 May

Constitution Day 3 May

Pentecost Sunday Seventh Sunday after Easter

Corpus Christi Ninth Thursday after Easter

Assumption Day 15 August

All Saints' Day 1 November

Independence Day 11 November

Christmas 25 and 26 December

Safe Travel

Kraków is a relatively low-crime city and you're not likely to experience serious problems. Pickpocketing and petty theft, however, remain rife, especially around the main tourist attractions. Keep valuables out of reach and be alert in crowds and on public transport. If you are the victim of a pickpocket, report the crime as soon as possible at any nearby police station.

Telephone

Domestic & International Calls

➡ Poland's country code is ☎48.

➡ All telephone numbers, landline and mobile, have nine digits. It's not necessary to dial a ☎'0' before calling between cities within Poland. Simply dial the unique nine-digit number.

➡ This guide lists landlines as ☎12 345 6789, with the first two numbers corresponding to the former city code. Mobile phone numbers are listed as ☎123 456 789.

Money-Saving Tips

➡ Choose your main restaurant meal at lunch. Many restaurants offer specially discounted two- and three-course lunch menus.

➡ Take advantage of the many canteen-like restaurants around town, including student-oriented vegetarian restaurants and traditional Polish milk bars (*bar mleczny*), where filling meals can be had for around 20zł.

➡ Most museums set aside one day a week for free admission. Entry is free on Sundays to the many fine exhibitions affiliated with the National Museum in Kraków (www.mnk.pl).

➡ If you're planning on using trams extensively, purchase the heavily discounted 24-, 48- and 72-hour passes instead of individual tickets.

➡ To call abroad from Poland, dial the international access code [↗](00), then the country code, then the area code and number. To dial Poland from abroad, dial your country's international access code, then 48 and then the nine-digit local number.

Mobile/Cell Phones

➡ Poland uses the GSM 900/1800 network, the same as the rest of Europe, Australia and New Zealand. This isn't compatible with most mobile phones in North America or Japan.

➡ A cheap option is to buy a local prepaid SIM card. They sell for as little as 10zł and can be organised quickly and painlessly. Before purchasing a SIM card, be sure your phone is unlocked (able to accept foreign SIM cards).

➡ The situation is more complicated for smartphones like an iPhone or Android device that may not be easily unlocked to accommodate a local SIM. With these phones, contact your home provider to consider short-term international calling and data plans appropriate to what you might need.

➡ Smartphones can be used as wi-fi devices, but switch your phone to 'airplane' mode on arrival, which blocks out calls and texts. Turn off 'data roaming' to avoid high roaming fees.

Toilets

➡ Toilets are labelled 'toaleta' or simply 'WC'.

➡ Men should look for 'dla panów' or 'męski', or a door marked by an upside-down triangle.

➡ Women should head for 'dla pań' or 'damski', or a door marked with a circle.

➡ The fee for a public toilet is 2zł, collected by a toilet attendant sitting at the door. Have small change ready.

Tourist Information

➡ The official tourist information office, **InfoKraków** (www.infokrakow.pl), maintains branches around town, including at the **Cloth Hall** (Map p46, C5; [↗]12 433 7310; Cloth Hall, Rynek Główny 1/3; ⊙9am-7pm May-Sep, to 5pm Oct-Apr; 🛜; 🚌1, 6, 8, 13, 18), **Kazimierz** (Map p68, E3; [↗]12 422 0471; ul Józefa 7; ⊙9am-5pm; 🚌6, 8, 10, 13), **Old Town** (Map p46, C4; [↗]12 421 7787; ul Św Jana 2; ⊙9am-7pm; 🚌1, 6, 8, 13, 18) and the

Dos & Don'ts

Fashion For sightseeing in Kraków, casual, comfortable clothing is the norm. Dress up for the opera or an evening out at a nice restaurant (a jacket for men, a skirt or pants suit for women). Smarten up for clubs to get by the bouncer at the door.

Churches Show respect when visiting churches. Speak in hushed tones and refrain from flash photography. Modest dress is preferred (long pants and covered shoulders). Never sight-see during mass.

Public Transport Don't block the door on crowded trams. Always yield your seat to an elderly or disabled person or expectant mother.

Airport (📞12 285 5341; www.en.infokrakow.pl; John Paul II International Airport, Balice; 🕐9am-7pm).

➡ Expect cheerful service, loads of free maps and promotional materials, help in sorting out accommodation and transport.

Travellers with Disabilities

➡ Kraków is generally not well equipped for people with disabilities, even though there has been a significant improvement over recent years.

➡ Wheelchair ramps are available only at some upmarket hotels and restaurants, and public transport will be a challenge for anyone with mobility problems.

➡ There are several useful websites for travellers with disabilities. If your Polish is up to snuff, try www.niepelnosprawni.pl for up-to-date information on the current situation.

Visas

➡ Citizens of EU countries do not need visas to visit Poland and can stay indefinitely. Citizens of the USA, Canada, Australia, New Zealand and many other countries can stay in Poland for up to 90 days without a visa.

➡ Other nationalities should check current visa requirements with the Polish embassy or consulate in their home country.

➡ There's more information on the **Polish Ministry of Foreign Affairs** (www.msz.gov.pl) website.

Language

Poland is linguistically one of the most homogeneous countries in Europe – more than 95% of the population has Polish as their first language. Polish belongs to the Slavic language family, with Czech and Slovak as close relatives. It has about 45 million speakers.

Vowels are generally pronounced short, giving them a 'clipped' quality. Note that **a** is pronounced as the 'u' in 'cut', **ai** as in 'aisle' and **ow** as in 'cow'. If you read the pronunciation guides in this chapter as if they were English you'll be understood just fine. Note that stressed syllables are indicated with italics.

English and German are widely understood in central Kraków, at least at hotels, restaurants and attractions frequented by foreign tourists. Transport staff and shop workers are more likely to only speak Polish.

To enhance your trip with a phrasebook, visit **lonelyplanet.com**.

Basics

Hello.
Cześć.   cheshch

Goodbye.
Do widzenia.   do vee·dze·nya

Yes./No.
Tak./Nie.   tak/nye

Please./You're welcome.
Proszę.   *pro*·she

Thank you.
Dziękuję.   jyen·*koo*·ye

Excuse me./Sorry.
Przepraszam.   pshe·*pra*·sham

How are you?
Jak pan/pani   yak pan/*pa*·nee
się miewa? (m/f)   shye *mye*·va

Fine. And you?
Dobrze.   *dob*·zhe
A pan/pani? (m/f)   a pan/*pa*·nee

Do you speak English?
Czy pan/pani   chi pan/*pa*·nee
mówi po   *moo*·vee po
angielsku? (m/f)   po an·*gyel*·skoo

I don't understand.
Nie rozumiem.   nye ro·*zoo*·myem

What's your name?
Jak się pan/   yak shye *pa*·na/
pani nazywa?   *pa*·nee na·*zi*·va
(m/f)

My name is ...
Nazywam się ...   na·*zi*·vam shye...

Eating & Drinking

I'd like the menu, please.
Proszę o   *pro*·she o
jadłospis.   ya·*dwo*·spees

I don't eat meat
Nie jadam mięsa   nye *ya*·dam *myen*·sa

Cheers!
Na zdrowie!   na *zdro*·vye

Please bring the bill.
Proszę o   *pro*·she o
rachunek.   ra·*khoo*·nek

Shopping

I'd like to buy ...
Chcę kupić ...   khtse *koo*·peech ...

I'm just looking.
Tylko oglądam.   *til*·ko o·*glon*·dam

How much is it?
Ile to kosztuje?   ee·le to kosh·*too*·ye

That's too expensive.
To jest za drogie.   to yest za *dro*·gye

Can you lower the price?
Czy może pan/   chi *mo*·zhe pan/
pani obniżyć   *pa*·nee ob·*nee*·zhich
cenę? (m/f)   *tse*·ne

Emergencies

Help!
Na pomoc!   na *po*·mots

Go away!
Odejdź!   o·deyj

Call the police!
Zadzwoń po   zad·zvon' po
policję!   po·*lee*·tsye

Call a doctor!
Zadzwoń po   zad·zvon' po
lekarza!   le·*ka*·zha

I'm lost.
Zgubiłem/   zgoo·*bee*·wem/
am się. (m/f)   wam shye

I'm ill.
Jestem   *yes*·tem
chory/a. (m/f)   *kho*·ri/ra

Where are the toilets?
Gdzie są toalety?   gjye som to·a·*le*·ti

Time & Numbers

What time is it?
Która jest   *ktoo*·ra yest
godzina?   go·*jee*·na

It's one o'clock.
Pierwsza.   *pyerf*·sha

Half past (10).
Wpół do   fpoow do
(jedenastej).   (ye·de·*nas*·tey)

morning
rano   *ra*·no

afternoon
popołudnie   po·po·*wood*·nye

evening
wieczór   *vye*·choor

yesterday
wczoraj   *fcho*·rai

today
dziś/dzisiaj   jeesh/*jee*·shai

tomorrow
jutro   *yoo*·tro

1	*jeden*	*ye*·den
2	*dwa*	dva
3	*trzy*	tshi
4	*cztery*	*chte*·ri
5	*pięć*	pyench
6	*sześć*	sheshch
7	*siedem*	*shye*·dem
8	*osiem*	*o*·shyem
9	*dziewięć*	*jye*·vyench
10	*dziesięć*	*jye*·shench

Transport & Directions

Where's a/the ...?
Gdzie jest ...?   gjye yest ...

What's the address?
Jaki jest adres?   *ya*·kee yest *ad*·res

Can you show me (on the map)?
Czy może pan/   chi *mo*·zhe pan/
pani mi   *pa*·nee mee
pokazać   po·*ka*·zach
(na mapie)? (m/f)   (na *ma*·pye)

When's the next (bus)?
Kiedy jest   *kye*·di yest
następny   nas·*temp*·ni
(autobus)?   (ow·*to*·boos)

A ... ticket (to Katowice).
Proszę bilet   *pro*·she *bee*·let
... (do Katowic).   ... (do ka·*to*·veets)

Behind the Scenes

Send Us Your Feedback

We love to hear from travellers – your comments help make our books better. We read every word, and we guarantee that your feedback goes straight to the authors. Visit **lonelyplanet.com/contact** to submit your updates and suggestions.

Note: We may edit, reproduce and incorporate your comments in Lonely Planet products such as guidebooks, websites and digital products, so let us know if you don't want your comments reproduced or your name acknowledged. For a copy of our privacy policy visit lonelyplanet.com/privacy.

Our Readers

Many thanks to the travellers who used the last edition and wrote to us with helpful hints, useful advice and interesting anecdotes:

Adele Reilly, Andy Stephens, Clare Brown, Denise O'Sullivan, Dirk Steinbock, Helen Claydon, Konrad Szarkowski, Łukasz Szymański, Melanie Luangsay, Poul Møller, Rowland Thomas, Tony Gordon

Mark's Thanks

I would like to thank my friends Olga Brzezińska and Magdalena Krakowska for taking the time to show me parts of their beautiful city.

Acknowledgments

Cover photograph: Rynek Główny, the main market square in Kraków; David Noton/Alamy

This Book

This 2nd edition of Lonely Planet's *Pocket Kraków* was researched and written by Mark Baker. This guidebook was produced by the following:

Destination Editor Gemma Graham **Product Editors** Grace Dobell, Elizabeth Jones, Katie O'Connell **Regional Senior Cartographer** Valentina Kremenchutskaya **Book Designer** Mazzy Prinsep **Assisting Editors** Samantha Forge, Jodie Martire **Cover Researcher** Brendan Dempsey **Thanks to** Andi Jones, Kate Kiely, Anne Mason, Karyn Noble, Kirsten Rawlings, Alison Ridgway, Angela Tinson, Lauren Wellicome, Tony Wheeler

Index

Sights p000
Map Pages **p000**

Our Writer

Mark Baker

Prague-based journalist and freelance writer Mark Baker first visited Poland as a student in the mid-1980s while the country was still part of the Eastern bloc and has returned many times over the years. He has worked as a writer and editor for the Economist Group, Bloomberg News and Radio Free Europe/Radio Liberty. In addition to contributing to the Lonely Planet guide to Poland and writing LP's pocket guide to Kraków, he's the author of Lonely Planet guides to Prague and the Czech Republic, Romania and Bulgaria, Slovenia, and the Baltic countries.

Published by Lonely Planet Publications Pty Ltd
ABN 36 005 607 983
2nd edition – February 2016
ISBN 978 1 74360 702 2
© Lonely Planet 2016   Photographs © as indicated 2016
10 9 8 7 6 5
Printed in Malaysia